slow
down

Also by David Essel

Books

Language for the Heart & Soul: Powerful Writings on Life

Papa's Amazing Tales: Diamond the Dolphin

Phoenix Soul: One Man's Search for Love & Inner Peace

The Real Life Adventures of Catherine "Cat" Calloway, The First

Audio Programs

Balancing Act: Create an Inspiring Life Mentally, Physically & Spiritually

Fit to Travel: 101 Tips to Stay Healthy and
Stress Free on the Road or at Home

How to Break Through Your Mental Barriers for Success

How to Stay Mentally Fit and Incredibly Productive

Living a Powerful Life in an Unbalanced World

No More Stress: A Relaxation and Meditation Program
for Your Health and Happiness

Phoenix Soul: One Man's Search for Love & Inner Peace

Stress Free: Master Life's Challenges to Create an Energetic Existence

Please visit Hay House USA: **www.hayhouse.com**
Hay House Australia: **www.hayhouse.com.au**
Hay House UK: **www.hayhouse.co.uk**
Hay House South Africa: **orders@psdprom.co.za**

Words of Praise for David Essel

*"David Essel's destiny is to help you become
more alive in every area of your life."*
— **Dr. Wayne W. Dyer,** the best-selling author
of *The Power of Intention* and
10 Secrets for Success and Inner Peace

"I love it! You are very talented and bright and insightful."
— **Jenna Elfman,** actress (*Dharma & Greg*)

*"All aspects of my life have been positively affected by the
work I've done with David. With his knowledge and
insights, he has helped me to build on my strengths and focus
on specific goals. He's a positive, motivating influence."*
— **Barbara,** lifestyle coaching client

*"You have awakened my soul! I can't seem to turn off, and I feel
alive again for the first time in four years. You are truly a very
caring soul. You really listen and look for the right answers to help
people. I feel that I am finally on my way to my life's goal."*
— **Ardith,** lifestyle coaching client

*"It has been several months since you addressed our sales force,
and our employees are still quoting you. In an age of information
overload, having such a lasting impact is truly impressive."*
— **Misti Bryant,** Nestlé Corporation

*"David is a genius at awakening your genius with a story.
This book is written in the spirit of the Hans Christian Anderson
stories and destined to become a classic."*
— author **Mark Victor Hansen,** on David's children's book
The Real Life Adventures of Catherine "Cat" Calloway, The First

*"David's powerful and results-oriented work
has helped me immensely. He has shown through his
coaching model that I can accomplish all that I desire
by simply reflecting back to me what I already know to be
true. He is a master at helping people to get results. Period."*
— **Lee Witt,** The Boeing Company

"Words are inadequate to describe my gratitude to you for your service to TEC 2062. The energy that you brought to the room was contagious. Your stories and examples brought the principles of effective relationships to our real lives. The members of TEC 2062 talked about your presentation all day and particularly mentioned how much they appreciated your candor and passion. Everyone gained a new understanding of more effective communications, and I am sure you contributed to many spirited conversations among couples in the group. You are truly the master of 'Real Life.'"
— **Skip Everitt,** TEC (The Executive Committee), Worldwide Network of CEOs (TEC stands for "The Executive Committee." It's a worldwide network of CEOs working together in small groups to support each other.)

"I happened to catch a portion of David's television show and realized instantly that he had the wisdom, judgment, and capacity to assist me with a difficult relationship issue. David possesses a wonderfully rare blend of strength and sensitivity. As a professional in a demanding career path, I was drawn to his energetic and efficient approach. For those who are either not in need of or not interested in the traditional counseling paradigm, David presents a powerful and unique alternative. For those committed to their own positive development and honest self-healing, David's method provides a helpful and effective framework to better enable success. I am unaware of any job description that would capture all that David does for his clients, but perhaps an apt job title would be '1:1 trainer for the heart and soul.'"
— **David,** attorney

✳ ✳ ✳

slow down

The Fastest Way to Get Everything You Want

David Essel

HAY HOUSE, INC.
Carlsbad, California
London • Sydney • Johannesburg
Vancouver • Hong Kong

Published and distributed in the United States by: Hay House, Inc., P.O. Box 5100, Carlsbad, CA 92018-5100 • *Phone:* (760) 431-7695 or (800) 654-5126 • *Fax:* (760) 431-6948 or (800) 650-5115 • www.hayhouse.com • **Published and distributed in Australia by:** Hay House Australia Pty. Ltd., 18/36 Ralph St., Alexandria NSW 2015 • *Phone:* 612-9669-4299 • *Fax:* 612-9669-4144 • www.hayhouse.com.au • **Published and distributed in the United Kingdom by:** Hay House UK, Ltd. • Unit 62, Canalot Studios • 222 Kensal Rd., London W10 5BN • *Phone:* 44-20-8962-1230 • *Fax:* 44-20-8962-1239 • www.hayhouse.co.uk • **Published and distributed in the Republic of South Africa by:** Hay House SA (Pty), Ltd., P.O. Box 990, Witkoppen 2068 • *Phone/Fax:* 2711-7012233 • orders@psdprom.co.za • **Distributed in Canada by:** Raincoast • 9050 Shaughnessy St., Vancouver, B.C. V6P 6E5 • *Phone:* (604) 323-7100 • *Fax:* (604) 323-2600

Design: Tricia Breidenthal

Library of Congress Cataloging-in-Publication Data

Essel, David
    Slow down: the fastest way to get everything you want / David Essel.
       p. cm.
    ISBN 1-40190-083-6 (tradepaper)
    1. Conduct of life. 2. Quality of life. I. Title.
BF637.C5 E386 2003
158—dc21
    2002007711

ISBN 1-4019-0083-6

07 06 05 04   4 3 2 1
1st printing, April 2004

Printed in the United States of America

I dedicate this book with <u>all of my love</u> to my mom and dad, Pat and Ed Essel. It was during the writing of this book that I came to see more clearly the power of my love for them, and of their love for me.

Contents

Foreword

A month ago, David Essel's assistant reminded me that I'd agreed to write this Foreword, and they needed it soon. I remember feeling annoyed by what seemed to be yet another imposition on my personal writing time, and vexed by my lifelong inability to refuse a friend any favor.

David is a friend. He's also one of the most decent, creative men I know. Keep in mind, I hadn't yet read *Slow Down*; I didn't know the energizing experience that awaited. So I was aggravated, and I made a private, familiar vow: *From now on, I will always say no. Always.*

I'd received the reminder via e-mail on my first night home after 39 days on a nonstop promotional tour for my new novel. The next morning I would be flying to New Orleans—ten more days on the road. So I desperately wanted to spend this lone evening kicking back on the porch of my old house. I'd missed the place (you would, too). You see, I live on an island on Florida's gulf coast, in a wooden house built in the 1920s. It's painted yellow, with a tin roof. The house sits on the remains of a shell pyramid that was inhabited for more than a thousand years by the indigenous people of our coast, the Calusa. The house has a screened, wraparound porch where, in the morning (when obligations allow), I sit and write.

I love the fact that for more than ten centuries, men and women have occupied my precise writing space, doing what I still attempt to do: tell stories. Increasingly, though, I spend less and less time on my porch. These days, the most difficult thing about writing is finding *time* to write. On the day of my return, the day I received the e-mail, I'd already come to deeply resent this reality.

So here's how my mini-retreat went: Leaving the airport, I received calls from my two much-loved sons. My oldest had been in a minor car wreck (he was unhurt, but certain insurance forms required attention). My youngest told me that I needed to contact the island fire department ASAP because my retrievers had escaped, and were last seen swimming toward Campeche. Madness.

I dealt with both problems on the way to the book signing for which I'd returned. The signing started at 4 P.M., and it was supposed to end at 5:30, so I could spend most of the evening at home. Instead, I signed books nonstop for nearly four hours. The store owner had risked her energy and capital, many people had gone to the trouble to come, so it was the least I could do.

Finally, at sunset, I arrived home—to find the yard grown to a jungle, the water shut off, my refrigerator empty, my car battery dead, and mail stacked in crates. Pals were on their way with beer and jumper cables, so while I waited, I opened a couple dozen letters from organizations, editors, writers, and friends I recognized. Most began with a variation on this theme: "I know you're busy, but if you get a little spare time, could you write . . . or blurb . . . or critique . . . or read . . . or speak . . . or sign a few dozen books?" Spare time? A few began, "Just want to remind you of that our deadline is fast approaching . . ."

I thought, *What about my deadlines? What about my writing? What about my life's work?* I hadn't been able to write a word while on the road. One note began: "I sent you 20 bookplates to sign more than a month ago, including return postage. I'm tired of waiting. Please return my postage." I hadn't been home in six weeks, and I hadn't had a private daylight minute to myself during the tour. I crumpled the letter, threw it across the room, and stomped out onto the porch, furious.

I was exhausted. I felt overwhelmed by what seemed like a strengthening implosion of demands that were draining me of my strength. I had a novel to finish, plus the Introduction to my new collection of essays, then a journal, which had been contracted but not even started. Alone on the porch, I tried to calculate how I could satisfy everyone plus get my own work done. Impossible. No way.

A writer's life is singular, solitary. A blank page can't be delegated, nor can a written word. Each and every small thing I do, I have to do alone. Yet success had so amplified my life's orbit that my life was now complicated beyond control. I looked at the boxes of mail, the unread scripts, and I felt like bawling—like I was under attack, but there was no way to circle the wagons. As David knows, I'm normally among the most positive (although disorganized) of people. But now a dark and negative energy seemed to have collected around the waiting mail, my house, and me.

My friends arrived to celebrate my lone night home. They put the jumper cables on backwards, ruined the battery, and fried the engine's main fuse. A couple hours later, I confronted an intruder robbing my house, then spent the remainder of the night dealing with police. Awful.

Alone, finally, yet unable to sleep, I decided to check my e-mail, and found David's assistant's reminder about my introduction to *Slow Down*. Annoyed? That's putting it mildly. I'm a big fan of David Essel, but the pressure to meet yet another obligation could not have come at a worse time in my life. Or so I thought . . .

The next morning on the flight to New Orleans, my attitude still stormy, I began to read David's book. I read: "It's only when we slow down and evaluate who we are, where we are, and what we really want from this existence, that we can speed ahead and bring to us all that we desire." I read: "Slow down and concentrate on being grateful for all that's good in your life. Send a thought of gratitude to the one, two, or three powerful friends who are by your side today."

I read on: "The only way to feel really good about ourselves and to enhance our sense of personal power is to be true to who we are at all times. For many of us raised in a society that says we need to be liked by all people at all times, this can initially be a daunting challenge. But by slowing down, we can leave the old behavior behind and relish our newly found power."

During the flight, my stormy attitude calmed. I liked what I was reading. My friend David was helping me understand not only how I'd lost control of my own life but, more important, how I could regain control again. I was particularly struck by the passage where David describes an encounter between his radio producer, Greg Bell, and an author they'd both admired whom they were scheduled to interview on David's show that day. When Greg calls the author before the prescribed time, the author reacts as if it's an imposition—as if he's under attack. He behaves like a childish ass.

Unknowingly, my pal David was sending me a private and powerful warning. *Slow Down*, it turned out, couldn't have come into my hands at a better time. The same may be true for you. There are good things in this book, strong and honest and true. My life is the better for reading it.

Thank you, David Essel. I'm so glad I said yes.

— Randy Wayne White
Pineland, Florida

❈

[**Author's Note:** Randy Wayne White (**www.rwwhite.com**) is the best-selling author of 13 books, including a highly acclaimed 10-book series featuring marine biologist Doc Ford. He was named "one of the hottest new writers in America" by *Booklist* magazine for his first novel in the Doc Ford series, *Sanibel Flats*, which was also chosen for the "100 Favorite Mysteries of the Century" by the Independent Mystery Booksellers Association. Randy also writes for *Men's Health* and *Men's Journal* magazines, and is a monthly columnist for *Outside* magazine.

I've loved each and every book that Randy has written, which is why I asked him to write the Foreword to my book. In my often hectic and harried life, Randy's novels are the ones that sit on my nightstand, helping me to slow down through the enjoyment of the powerful mysteries he has created.]

❈ ❈ ❈

How to Use This Book to Reap the Rewards of Slowing Down

What does it mean to slow down? Well, for starters, when we're living a life in the slow lane, we live with gratitude for what we have, instead of wishing life would always be different. We become more aware of the good things in this world, which not only adds a sense of inner peace to our existence, but also enhances our energy so that we can begin living each day in a more abundant way. Slowing down opens our eyes to the real world that revolves around us so that we can make a more conscious daily effort to assist others who may be in need of a simple smile or kind word of encouragement. Slowing down means getting out of the mundane life that so many of us live in and moving on to one filled with more hope, optimism, and energy.

When we slow down, we become more aware of *all* the emotions we're feeling on a daily basis—not just the ones we label as "good." By acknowledging all our frustration, anger, jealousy, and insecurities, they begin to loosen their grip on us, and we move to a more centered place and enjoy a more balanced life.

By slowing down, we can live more consciously and take more control of our existence, thereby realizing that we have more power than we could have ever imagined—and letting go of the many preconceived notions of how we should be living our lives. We can access the inner knowledge that helps us find true happiness, which up to this point may have been elusive.

WHY WE ALL NEED TO SLOW DOWN

The principles in this book are life transforming. If you're finally ready to get all you want out of life, you've come to the right place—for it's only when you slow down and evaluate *who* you are, *where* you are, and *what* you really want from this existence that you can speed ahead and bring all that you desire into your life.

In today's world, we're all faced with the incredible pressure that "time-saving" technology was supposed to take care of. Computers, cell phones, and pagers were intended to make our lives easier. They didn't—instead, they stripped us of our downtime and added more stress to our existence. For these reasons alone, we *all* need to slow down. By doing so, we realize all the greatness that's in our lives even when we're struggling and in pain. We begin to cherish the life we have today, even if it doesn't seem to be turning out as we'd envisioned. When we slow down, we take less for granted and live more abundantly.

One of the most moving experiences from my radio-show days occurred during one of the many interviews I did with musician and author Meat Loaf. He recalled a story that shook me to my core and made me realize more than ever that I need to live with joy every moment that I'm alive.

While at a record-signing event that lasted for hours, a couple came up to meet Meat Loaf and asked for his autograph. The woman seemed shy, and the singer could tell that there was something on the young man's mind as well. Well, the man told Meat Loaf that his music had saved his girlfriend's life. She had gone to a hotel room, put a pistol in her mouth, and just as she was about to pull the trigger, Meat Loaf's song "Heaven Can Wait" came on the radio. It moved her so deeply that she slowed down and removed the gun from her mouth. She realized that even though she was in deep pain, her life still had great value.

REAPING THE REWARDS OF SLOWING DOWN

The practice of slowing down has brought more into my life, as well as the lives of my life-coaching clients, than I ever imagined possible. Personally, I've had financial success that I never thought I'd see; I've created and experienced fantastic, loving relationships with women who have taught me much more than I ever dreamed possible; and I've experienced a deepening of my faith and my spiritual path in ways I never believed could have happened. By slowing down and listening to my intuitive voice—the same strong voice that you have, too—I've created career paths without any formal training, I've watched my physique change in ways that I always desired, and I've found an immense well of creativity within me. Every lesson and every success that I've encountered can be attributed to the concept of slowing down.

Now it's your turn to experience the same successes that my clients and I have witnessed. While there are many books on goal setting, this one is unique, for in my process I'll teach you how to go after all that you desire while at the same time letting go of the end result you think you need. By doing so, you'll feel less stressed and more empowered, and all that you desire will come into your life—with less effort on your part.

How I Began to Slow Down

I've used the concept of slowing down over the past 12 years to help countless people. I've also applied these principles with enormous success to my own life, and to prove how effective this program is, throughout this book I'll share with you what happened to me when I *didn't* slow down.

In one way or another, I've been practicing and writing about this life philosophy for nearly 20 years, but I began to seriously follow the process of slowing down when I was the host of my radio show. The program, *David Essel—Alive!*, was syndicated in more than 220 cities every Saturday and Sunday, and brought information about health, personal growth, relationships, and spirituality to millions of listeners. During that time, I was also working as a lifestyle coach. As such, I would assist clients from all over the country in their search for success, peace, and happiness. From the very beginning, I could see that the more my clients slowed down, the more success they achieved in every area of their lives. As they executed the writing exercises I gave them after each session, they were able to access the information inside themselves that allowed them to make better decisions. Whether they were trying to figure out what career path they should take or decide if they should stay in a love relationship, my clients were all using the knowledge that resided within to help them quickly move ahead in life. I was ecstatic to see this happening to each and every one of them, and I could clearly see the reason for their success: They were all slowing down and listening to their inner guide. And, when they coupled this with the act of meditation, their results and the answers they were seeking were coming at an even faster pace.

In my own life, I was also moving ahead, feeling that my purpose for being here was growing deeper every day—yet I was pushing too hard and working too many hours. I wanted to live a life full of love and inner peace, so I decided to follow my own advice. I wanted to slow down, and I knew I'd have to let go of my need to achieve, achieve, and achieve some more. But could I do less and still feel connected to people and my goals? I quieted my ego, which had been telling me that to be *really* successful, I had to keep accomplishing more. I began meditating and praying more each day, and I began to clearly see that it was time to move from my beautiful beach home to a new city for fresh adventures, lessons, and opportunities to grow. I decided to let go of doing anything other than the weekend radio show. And slowing down brought me back to my true self.

Then, when my professional life began to unravel due to events that were totally out of my control, I immediately saw how powerful the slowing-down process really was. I received a call one day from my radio syndicator telling me that the company was cancelling all live weekend talk shows, and that I'd soon be out of a job. I was stunned. My show had been a success for nine straight years—how could they end it? I had just signed a two-year contract extension that included a raise a few months before this call. How could they back out now? Apparently they had found an escape clause in my contract, so I had no option but to move on.

I missed my audience deeply. Yet unlike in the past, where I would have let this loss devastate me, I was able to see that there was a reason for all that was occurring. Because my faith and trust in life had been strengthened so deeply through the act of slowing down, I was able to recover quickly. Of course it's normal to become paralyzed when an event like this happens, but the principles of slowing down prepared me for this loss by showing me that who I *am* is much more important than what I *do*.

How Slowing Down Is the Fastest Way to Get Everything You Want

It does seem like an oxymoron, doesn't it? At first, it doesn't make sense that the fastest way to get everything you want can only occur if you're willing to slow down—yet it's so very true. Let me explain why.

Through the slowing-down process, you're able to think more deeply and more clearly, which enables you to make better decisions—with respect to your career path, your physical body, and your love relationships—so you get on the right path to your goals more quickly.

When you slow down, you may find that what you *thought* you always wanted and what you *really* want may be two different things. Some of my clients who initially thought they needed a life partner or more money came to realize that what they really desired was a way to express and enhance their purpose here on Earth. This reminds me of the movie *A Civil Action*. As a high-powered and wealthy attorney, the main character believed that he'd found his path to success in life. Little did he know how radically his definition of success would change. After losing all his money and possessions, which he had invested in a civil-action suit, he's left with $14 to his name. In a letter he writes to a fellow attorney, he says that according to all commonly held definitions of success, he's a failure. Yet if he had the opportunity to do it all over again—knowing all that he'd have to go through—he wouldn't change a thing. He knew that he was a success. You see, only when he slowed down could he evaluate his priorities in life. And when he did this, he found that fighting for a just cause was more rewarding to him than making lots of money.

The same may happen to you. Slow down and you'll reap the rewards of the life you desire.

THE POWER OF WRITING

You'll notice that unlike some books, I don't offer my own recap at the end of each chapter, stating what I believe the important points were in the preceding pages. This is because I want *you* to decide what's important in this book, not be spoon-fed what I think is relevant to your journey.

Experts in human growth (and I agree with them) have known for centuries that to truly get ahead in life, it helps to write down your desires, strengths, and challenges. Breakthroughs occur when you take the time to write, even if it's just briefly answering one of the many introspective questions posed throughout this book. Why? Because you can think and speak much faster than you can write. Writing slows you down, allowing your inner wisdom to rise to the surface. The answers you're seeking today about love, money, your health, or even what your life purpose is all reside within you, and by doing some brief writing exercises, you'll be closer to finding them.

Through this writing process, you can also access the blocks, or the negative beliefs, that have been holding you back. You'll see how to strip away your self-imposed myths and limitations and let them go so that you can honestly access the real goals you have for yourself.

Throughout this book, you'll find short writing exercises and questions that I'll ask you to fill in. Some may seem to be of little consequence to your current path, but please take a moment or two to slow down and fill in your answers. At the end of each part of the book, you'll also find a review area with several questions that relate to the material you just read. These questions come from my many years of work as a life and business coach. Simple yet powerful, they've helped each client I've worked with accomplish his or her individual goals. As all of my clients will attest, there's great wisdom and information to be gained by filling in the answers to these questions.

USING THIS BOOK TO MAXIMIZE YOUR SUCCESS

This book was designed to take you step-by-step along the path to personal success and life enrichment. You'll begin by looking at the three keys to manifesting what you desire in life, and end the book by reading about the power that lies within those who have a service-oriented mentality. In between, I'll help you explore ways to enhance your love relationships as well as deepen the spiritual side of your life, and you'll find all you'll need to live a life full of personal power and excellent health.

While I recommend that you read this book in the order that it's presented, if you happen to be struggling in any one of these specific areas and feel the need to go directly to that part, please feel free to do so. Each part has been created as a separate entity unto itself, allowing you the freedom to go where you need to at that moment.

YOUR NEW LIFE ADVENTURE IS ABOUT TO BEGIN

While adding the final touches to this book, I had the most remarkable conversation with Natasha Gerhart, an art media consultant, at one of her open houses in Florida. Natasha creates marketing plans for artists who want to show their work in the hopes of making their passion a full-time career. She was intrigued with the whole philosophy behind my concept of slowing down to find success, and told me: "What you're writing about is the crux, the centerpiece, for any artist who wants to be successful. It's not just talent that creates a career in art. The artist must slow down and see that they cannot let rejection or impatience rule their world. It's often not that the marketing plan is misdirected, it's that the artist needs to look at this as a lifelong goal, a lifelong love. If they do this, they'll ultimately be successful at what they love."

And so will you.

❊

As an aside, I'd just like to mention that throughout this book you'll read about several of my past and present clients, and you'll see how the principle of slowing down helped them accomplish their most important goals. You'll see how Lee, Sheryl, Jody, Lisa, John, David, and others maximized their potential by using the same techniques that you're about to learn. I think you'll discover that we really are the same in so many ways: We're all searching for information to help us get in touch with our real needs, strengths, challenges, and goals. I know you'll get a lot out of the power that these individuals display in life.

So imagine right now that you're about to embark on the most exciting adventure of your lifetime—to uncover all that you truly can about life and yourself. Don't worry about what to pack for this trip, because you already have all that you need. Your mission, if you choose to accept it—your *mission possible*, if you will—is to slow down. This journey inward will transform you and allow you to get all that you want out of life in the shortest amount of time. Period. So slow down to finally discover *who* you truly are, *what* you really want, and *how* to make it happen.

❋ ❋ ❋

Slow Down

with the Three Keys

of Manifestation:

Intention,

Gratitude, and

Action

chapter 1

The Power of Intention

The cornerstones needed to live an abundant life are *intention*, *gratitude*, and *action*, or the three keys to manifestation. The beautiful thing about them is that it takes nothing more than a mental awareness of their importance to benefit from what they have to offer. It takes little or no physical energy on your part to see your life begin to change—all that's required is the simple act of acknowledgment to shift how you feel and even look.

The first thing you must do in order to manifest what you truly want is to create the *intention* to go after your goals. All change must begin with the desire to live life differently, yet how often do you slow yourself down enough to mentally move to a different place?

My client Amy learned about the power of intention after a romantic split. When she came to see me, she said that the breakup had begun to consume her thoughts. She found herself focusing on all that was going wrong in her world, which was causing her immense sadness and pain. I asked her to tell me how she'd advise a close friend in a similar situation, and Amy said that she'd ask her friend to begin to think about all the great blessings she had in this life.

"How do you jump from living day-to-day in pain to living in gratitude?" I asked. The answer was plain for Amy to see: She needed to create the intention to live each day of her life differently.

I asked Amy to write down a list of attributes that she'd like to experience in her life right away. She came up with several, including peace, deep faith in God and His path for her, a loving relationship, and a sense of thankfulness for all that she had. She began to recognize the interconnectedness of several of her goals—for example, she realized that her wish for greater inner peace was tied in to her desire for a deeper faith in God, as well as her longing to live a life full of gratitude. These intentions became a part of her daily life.

Author Wayne Dyer tells a similar story about how he created the daily intention to stop drinking alcohol. His intention was that *this* day would be alcohol free, and that mental work would manifest his sobriety. He referred to himself as a camel who began and ended each day on his knees and could go 24 hours without a drink.

How *you* create success in any area of life may very well be different from how someone else does it, but the one common thread is that you must *slow down* daily and create the intention for change to occur.

DAILY INTENTIONS

Most people view the use of intentions as an important way to go after the "big stuff" in life. But what about the intentions that can be used to make each day more enjoyable? I once spoke to a roundtable of CEOs about the power of intention. I took the opportunity to go into detail about the use of smaller daily intentions such as, "I intend to pay more attention to the flowers and trees on the way to work today," "I intend to be more patient in traffic," and "I intend to give more compliments everywhere I go."

A few days later, I received an e-mail from one of the executives who'd been at the meeting. He said, "Words can't describe what your presentation did for me. I've needed to slow down for years, to pay attention to all that's around me. Creating the intention each morning to look for beauty in nature as I drive to work has put a smile on my face and a spark in my day. Thank you."

How would you like your life to change? If you slow down enough to create the daily intention to connect with what you desire, it can become your reality. You see, your intention is the spark that lights the fire to help you change your life. Without it, it's a tough shift to go from struggle to gratitude. For example, to go from pain and disillusionment when it comes to finding deep love with a partner to actually experiencing that love takes a conscious effort on your part—an intention that says you're ready for such a beautiful thing to occur. Simply put, creating a daily list of intentions slows you down and makes you more conscious about how you live your life.

Take a moment and create a list of intentions that you'd like to see manifested in your life by completing the following sentence: "I intend to create the following in my life [for example, *inner peace, sobriety, greater health, more money, the career path of your dreams, deeper love,* and so on]:"

Look over your list of intentions and pick out the one that would have the greatest impact on your life once brought to fruition. Circle it, and for the next 60 days, stay highly focused on this one goal. Now, like Amy, Wayne Dyer, and thousands of other successful people, every morning when you wake up just lie in bed for a moment and concentrate on the intention you want to manifest in your life—whatever you desire. Then throughout the day, as you're driving or walking, for instance, bring your intention to mind. Your thoughts set into motion the energy needed to keep you focused on what you wish to bring into your life.

As my brother, Terry, would say, "Through the use of our intentions, we're simply keeping our most important thoughts on the front burner." And it's true. Your heightened awareness may lead you to individuals who can help you achieve your goal—people you may not have paid attention to otherwise. Or perhaps the circulating energy you send off when you're living a more focused life will bring people who have helped you in the past back into the fold to assist you in your quest today. But it does take a willingness to slow your life down, even just a little, to make this happen. In just seconds per day, you can refocus your life by bringing to mind your intention to change.

CREATING POWERFUL AND EFFECTIVE INTENTIONS

Before you get too specific about creating your intentions, take a look at the different ways these thoughts can be written. I believe that the most effective ones are specific, yet open-ended at the same time. This may sound contradictory at first, but it really does make a lot of sense.

One of my clients created a list of intentions that she wanted to manifest in every area of her life. When she reached the one about her career goals, she wrote that she wanted to "expand my energies and talents in a position that would challenge me mentally and stimulate me creativity, allowing me to maximize my computer and artistic abilities." This was all fantastic, but then she specifically listed the name of the company that she wanted to work for. This is where she got tripped up by good intentions, so to speak.

I mentioned to her that when we get too specific, we risk getting so narrowly focused that we may bypass other great possibilities that come knocking at our door because we're only looking for this one opportunity. As my client sat blindly waiting for a call from one company, she might miss her own intuitive voice screaming to her to be open to other options—options that could prepare her for her future work. I advised my client that maybe she needed to work with two or three other companies to acquire the skills she'd need to be truly ready to work with this particular organization. Or maybe she was meant to go in a totally different and more fulfilling direction. Creating an intention that's too limited or specific may actually take you off of your path instead of leading you down it.

With respect to relationships, the same holds true. For example, the idea of welcoming a wonderful man into your life who's six feet tall, athletic, artistic, successful, has dark hair and green eyes, loves children, and is patient may make your heart flutter. But what if an amazing man who *doesn't* fit these characteristics is sitting right next to you? What if this man could bring you joy and help you grow to reach your full potential like no other? And what if he happened to be blond, nerdy, and 5'7"? If you become too specific, you might just miss the real deal. Here's a story that illustrates this point.

I once met a woman who told me that for years she'd been complaining to her friends that there were no good men available to date—she was sure that the supply of male life partners was diminishing. At 38, she was bitter about being alone and pessimistic about her future. She'd read a book on relationships that said people should be very specific about the type of partner they were searching for, the theory being that you bring into your life the type of people you think about most often. Yet regardless of how many times the woman created her specific intention, she never seemed to find her ideal mate.

This same woman had been friends for several years with a certain guy, but she never saw him as a romantic partner. And although he wasn't her type physically, she loved to be around him because he made her laugh. He'd never shown any romantic interest in her either, but once a week they'd meet for lunch to catch up on what was happening in each other's lives.

At one of these meetings, when the man was away from their table, another acquaintance walked over to the woman and asked her who the new man in her life was. "Oh, him?" the woman responded. "He's just a good friend." The acquaintance was quite surprised to hear this, and before she left said, "The chemistry between you two is very electric— you can easily see it from across the room. I'd look into that possibility a little deeper if I were you." With that, they laughed, and the acquaintance walked away.

The woman was surprised to hear such a comment about a guy who hadn't fit any of the physical requirements she'd written down in her search for a life partner. She'd become so focused on the details of height, weight, and so forth that she didn't pay attention to all the other attributes this person brought to the table. Over the next few days, she started to reflect on the other characteristics she was looking for in a partner. As she slowed down, she realized that what she really wanted was someone who was compassionate, caring, communicative, and funny—and her male friend scored hits in all these categories. She began to reevaluate all that she desired and how this person, who had been in front of her all this time, might be someone who could help her create the life she desired. Today, at age 50, she's happier than she's ever been with her husband and best friend. She can now laugh as she recalls the importance of slowing down to create an intention—without the details being *so specific* that they cloud your vision.

TRUSTING THE PATH TO MANIFESTATION

When I created my intention to move to a new place and follow a new path, I never would have consciously chosen a small city in the middle of Florida. But had I not trusted the end result of my intention and come to Gainesville, I never would have had the amazing friendships that opened me up to deeper love, or the opportunities that helped hone my television-hosting abilities. Had I said, "I intend to move to another warm beach town," I never would have had the chance to experience all that I did in this small Florida city. I'll be forever grateful for that experience, which proved to me that the best intentions truly are both general and specific.

A few years ago after my radio show ended, I kept my intentions highly focused on getting signed with another national program. Instead of trusting that there might be another path I should stay open to, I dug my heels in and tried to control where I'd work next. Finally, after trying to create my next radio opportunity for more than eight months, I totally let the intention go. My newly created intention was all about serving, with whatever God-given talents I had, in any way I could. I opened my intention up to go back into TV, public speaking, or whatever path was the right one for me.

Within 30 days of shifting my intention from one of rigidness to one of openness, an opportunity arose to do a TV pilot with Cox Communications in Gainesville. The goal was to syndicate this show through their 35 other cities if the base facility could organize their troops to get this done. I had to laugh as I realized that regardless of whether they syndicated the show or not, just the fact that my open intentions had led to this opportunity was quite amazing and very exciting!

My intentions then shifted to finding a publisher for a book I'd been writing, which had an underlying theme of love and spirituality. I kept my intentions open as several months went by. Then, from out of the blue, I received a call from Hay House, who wanted me to write my next book for them.

At that moment, I realized how powerful my intentions had become. I'd created a perfect match with a publisher: I had the utmost respect for Hay House founder Louise Hay—and the great work she'd been doing for years—and now I was being offered an opportunity that authors sometimes only dream about.

While not all intentions create contracts, I've found that the more you practice, the better your odds become. Within a month of the Cox TV deal, I received a call from an Emmy–award winning producer I hadn't talked to in more than ten years, Marsha Posner Williams. Marsha was calling to see if I'd be interested in joining her and Carl Lauten (whom I'd also worked with on an infomercial years before) in a potential TV show or video series on the mind, body, and spirit. Lucky coincidences? I don't think so. I see this as further proof that there's power in the daily use of intention.

✻

You too can start to slow down and manifest your dreams through the use of intentions. Here's what my client Sheryl had to say about the power of intention: "I've learned that by slowing down, creating an intention, and then sending that thought out to the universe, I can manifest results in a short period of time. The power of intention has helped me be more patient and more spiritual, and I've discovered creative and poetic sides to me that I never knew existed." Just like Sheryl, you can create all that you desire through the use of intention.

✻ ✻ ✻

chapter 2

The Power of Gratitude

The second key to manifesting all that you desire is to learn how to live with gratitude. I remember a time in my life when I was struggling in several areas. A new relationship that I had put an immense amount of love and emotion into had hit a serious wall. My career, which had been flourishing, had just crashed. Then, to top it all off, I lost a large amount of money in an investment I thought was a sure winner. I was spinning out of control, with my thoughts of "lack" consuming almost every moment.

After about two weeks of asking "Why me?" I decided to use a technique on myself that had worked beautifully for many of my clients who had hit tough times: I went back to thoughts of gratitude for all that I have. It sounds so easy, almost too simple to work—yet it does. I knew that I could manifest more peace in my life if I started filling my thoughts with thankfulness for all that I had: my patient and loving dog, Kona; my family, including my brother, who is always available to hear my pain; and one of my assistants, who is an amazingly levelheaded confidant. I even expressed my gratitude for the last meal I'd eaten and for a book I'd read about Mother Teresa.

One of the most basic tenets of a happy, successful life is that you become what you think about. So if your mind is full of thoughts of gratitude, you become more centered on what you *do* have instead of what you *don't* have. It's so easy to stay in a negative state when life is throwing challenge after challenge your way, yet this is the time you need to slow down and focus on all that you do have. As you do so, more often then not you'll see that you have so much to feel joyful about, and this realization will by itself manifest more joy and happiness.

Only you can shift your focus if you're willing to slow down enough to get to this place of gratitude, so take a moment to look at your life. Write down the areas that you might be struggling in, followed by all that you have to be grateful for. The process of slowing yourself down enough to focus on what you have may be just what you need to help you succeed.

- Use the following space to complete this sentence: "The challenges I face in life right now are related to my [*career, relationship, money, health*, and so on]":

_____

_____

_____

_____

- Now ask yourself the following question, and write your answer in the space provided. "What do I have that I'm grateful for in life?" (For example, *faith, food, shelter, relationships, health, or money,* to name a few.)

_____

_____

_____

_____

It's so easy to get wrapped up in all that's going wrong at any given moment, because it takes a lot less energy to focus on negatives rather than filling your mind with gratitude. That's why I ask my clients to write down a list of what they have to be grateful for on a daily basis. This technique, which only takes a few minutes to do, can have a powerful effect on your attitude. And the only way that you can manifest greatness and abundance in your life is if you change your mind-set, starting today.

Several times a day, without ignoring the challenges you face, focus your thoughts on all that you already have. Immerse yourself in your abundance to bring stronger, more positive energy into your life. Slow down enough to give this principle of success a chance, and you'll find that you can manifest what you desire by surrounding yourself with gratitude.

THANKING YOUR ANGELS

We often forget to tell the special people in our lives how important they are to us. When we do so, we often find that the boost these "angels" receive is immeasurable, and we feel so much better about ourselves for making someone else's day so much brighter.

- Take a moment to list the people who have made a difference in your life. You might include lovers, teachers, family members, your doctor or auto mechanic, co-workers, or a neighbor. Then jot yourself a note to call, e-mail, or mail them a letter, letting them know how important they are to you. Slow down and acknowledge your "angels" now with gratitude:

_____

_____

_____

_____

As I focus with gratitude on just a few of the people I have in my life, I can't help but feel a natural slowing down in my thoughts.

ACKNOWLEDGING YOUR GIFTS

Sometimes it's easier to be grateful for what others bring to your life than it is to be thankful for the special gifts you have within yourself. These are the talents given to you at—or some believe before—birth. How often do you acknowledge the gifts that you've been given? Unfortunately, many people may not even be aware that they have any special gifts at all.

From Trappist monk Thomas Merton to Nelson Mandela, from Joan of Arc to author Marsha Sinetar, through the ages the message of tapping in to your individual gifts and believing in yourself has been a central theme to living a life full of joy and connectedness. Helping others acknowledge their special gifts has become a passion of mine as I travel around the country reading the two children's books I've written, *The Real Life Adventures of Catherine "Cat" Calloway, The First*; and *Papa's Amazing Tales: Diamond the Dolphin*, to elementary school children. I ask them to go after their dreams and uncover their special gifts because we *all* have them. Regardless of our age, we all need to be grateful for who we are.

- Take a moment now and write down the gifts or talents that you've been given. You might have a great personality or sense of humor, athletic prowess, musical talent, a compassionate ear, artistic skills, or the ability to inspire people. List as many gifts as you can:

_____

_____

_____

_____

Now say a few words of gratitude, either to yourself or to God or a higher power, for all that you've been given and for all that you've developed on your own. If you don't slow down enough to see these gifts, you'll continue to live a life of partial joy. As you reflect on these talents with gratitude, your energy will increase and you'll be able to go out and make an even bigger difference in this world—which, ultimately, is the reason you're here.

But what do you do if you don't believe that you have any gifts or talents at all? Unfortunately, this happens all too often. Vicki was a client I worked with briefly in order to address this very subject. During our first session, she told me that she had "nothing to be grateful for." She hated her job, but because she'd decided that she had no talent or ability to do anything else, she was stuck. She asked me, "So what kind of magic do you think you can work with me?" I told her that the work I do is an inside job—that is, my clients have to go within and answer their own questions.

I was finally able to convince her to do the following exercise (and I'll ask you to do the same if you doubt your uniqueness in this world). I asked Vicki to call a close friend or two, a family member, or even a co-worker or neighbor who knew her well, and ask them to list what special abilities or personality traits they saw in her. It's often easier for others to see our gifts, especially when our thoughts are filled with lack and focused on all that we're not.

Vicki reluctantly agreed to do this, but said that she thought it was a total waste of her time. The following week, I wasn't a bit surprised to find out that the two people she had asked to give her their opinion of her gifts—a friend and a co-worker—had each listed many strong qualities they saw in Vicki. They both said that she was a great listener, she was empathetic to other people's problems, and she'd shown strong artistic talent in remodeling her home. Yet when I asked Vicki to consider what these people had seen as a sure sign of her talent, she scoffed at the suggestion and remained firm in her belief that she was destined to be unhappy working at the same office job for the rest of her life. After just a few sessions, Vicki cancelled her work with me.

You always have to make your own choices when it comes to moving forward or staying where you are. I hope that Vicki found her own path and has created a more settled and happy life, but this example proves what I've always known to be true: Manifesting a life that's more abundant and joyful than the one you currently have is a mental project. It all begins within your mind.

- If you struggle with the fact that you have special gifts or talents, then at the very least, make a commitment to your growth by calling a few people and asking for their opinion. Write their responses below:

Name	Relationship to Me	Response

Now, take a close look at your list. Is it time to begin to apply more of what you've been given in life? Is it time to go back to school or change careers so that you can maximize all that you are and make a real difference in your life and the world?

Slow down. Acknowledge with gratitude what others see in you. Then move ahead with gusto. Remember, you become what you think about. As you consider all that you have to be thankful for, you slowly become more grateful, optimistic, and energized. This is a key step in manifesting a more joyful and powerful existence.

❋ ❋ ❋

chapter 3

The Power of Action

The third key to manifesting what you desire in your life is to take action. I remember playing baseball as a kid for a coach who used to tell us, "You can't win if you don't show up at the plate." I don't remember that coach's name, and I'm sure I had no idea what the heck he was talking about back then, but what he said makes perfect sense to me today. After all, how can you expect to see changes in your life if you don't prove that you're serious about your intentions?

After you decide to change your life and surround yourself with gratitude, you have to demonstrate that you're willing to go after your goals. "Showing up at the plate" is the difference between the person who says that he wants to be an actor but spends all his time lamenting the fact that there aren't any good jobs available, and the one who enrolls in acting lessons anyway. The second person is truly taking action.

I often work with people who desire more confidence, a deeper connection with their true self, or higher self-esteem, and I know that regardless of past experiences or current situations, each and every one of us can have the life we want if we take the necessary steps. First, we must repeat the intentions we desire to create. Then, after reflecting with gratitude on all that we do have, we must take action. For example, to get better at shooting free throws, we must repeat that as our intention, be thankful for the skills we have, and then go to the gym and practice.

So what do you want out of life? And how will you show up at the plate to get it? The following is Jody's story about the power within all of us that's released when we move from intention to action.

> I'm a single mom, and there was a time when I was struggling to make ends meet. It seemed to me that life was an uphill struggle, and I was depressed. Then I heard David's talk-radio show one day and was immediately impressed by the advice he was giving. When I checked out his Website, I learned that he coached clients one-on-one, and after reading their testimonies, I knew that I had to find a way to work with him, too.
>
> I was desperate for help, but I couldn't afford David's fee, so I e-mailed him, explaining my circumstances and how much I wanted to work with him. His response was, "Pay what you can, and let's begin!"
>
> During our first session, David told me, "If we just show up, the universe responds tenfold." Since then, I've become convinced that more often than not, this is what happens when we take action in life. After all, I "showed up" by asking for help, and he responded.
>
> Of course it hasn't always been easy, and I sometimes find myself faced with many challenges. But after working with David, I could see that these roadblocks were orchestrated by the universe and aimed at helping me grow. With this understanding, each challenge I faced

became easier—even magical! I was able to face each one with the knowledge that whatever needed to happen would happen . . . and it did!

I came out of every situation with more power and inner knowing than I had at the onset. Now I'm a better mom and role model for my son, and a more content human being. I'm filled with gratitude!

SHOW UP AT THE PLATE IN YOUR LIFE TODAY

Let's slow down and look at some examples of showing up at the plate to create the life you desire.

— Clients often approach me for guidance in finding or maintaining relationships. If you're looking for romance, you might investigate dating services or let friends know that you're open to love. But people forget that the first step might simply be to leave an unhealthy relationship. So many of my clients have responded to this suggestion with an "Aha" look on their face—after all, it makes perfect sense: What action could prove more seriously to you and the universe that you're ready for true love than leaving a relationship that's not right for you?

— Do you want to become a public speaker? I remember a former mentor, Richard Gerson, giving me this great advice: Plan on speaking anywhere, to any group you can, on topics that you really enjoy. And in the beginning, plan on doing it for free if you must. That's showing up to the plate. For example, during the first year of my speaking career, I'd fly anywhere to speak, for expenses only. Then the next year, I'd ask for $200 plus expenses. My intention was to be the most incredible speaker that I could be, and I took action by doing it for free or a nominal fee. The practice and experience was invaluable, and it helped skyrocket my career.

— Do you want to get into great shape? Join a health club today, regardless of your fitness level. So many people say, "I'll join the gym once I lose a few more pounds." Of course they almost never join, and they never take the steps to get the body they've always wanted.

— Do you want to become wealthy? Start saving more money now, even before you get that next raise. Do you want to be an author? Then write your book—even before you find a publisher. If a contract doesn't come right away, write another one. Do you want to be surrounded by great, dynamic friends? Become a friend to others, starting today.

Live differently, and risk feeling embarrassed and looking out of place. To get what you want out of life, show up to the plate today.

Slow down now and complete the following sentences:

- The number-one goal I want to accomplish is . . .

_____

_____

- My intention, which I'll repeat daily, regarding this goal is . . .

_____

_____

Maybe your goal is to find a new job, so your intention could be something like, "Today I intend to find a new career path that will allow me to learn, grow, and maximize my potential in a fun, challenging, and extremely rewarding position." For you, taking action might mean looking at job listings online or in trade publications, and depending on your situation, it may also include giving your current employer your two-week notice.

Consider what it will take to prove that you're serious about your goal, and finish the following sentence:

- The steps I need to take to show up to the plate and achieve this goal are . . .

_____

_____

It's not enough to simply immerse yourself daily in gratitude or to create the intention to see your life change for the better. The action step is the third key to your success.

A good friend and former client of mine, Lee Witt, paid his own way through college while playing football at Illinois State University as a walk-on athlete. Here, in Lee's words, is the power of intention plus showing up to the plate:

The challenge of paying my way through college seemed terribly daunting to my 18 year-old-heart, but by simply putting one foot in front of the other, I paid every dime. I worked 84 hours a week during the summers for the Green Giant Company, I played in piano bars and coffeehouses, I ran study halls for the freshman football players, and I took out student loans. I even posed nude for art classes for $10 an hour. But I did it.

Now when I feel tired or frustrated, I think back to those days and remember that I can do whatever it takes to make something happen. It has become a great reference point for me—and a personal source of immense satisfaction.

Take a moment to complete the following exercise. By finishing these sentences, you'll gain a clear picture of what it will take to improve each aspect of your life, which will positively affect the whole of your existence.

Health

- I intend . . .

- My action step is . . .

Finances

- I intend . . .

_____

_____

- My action step is . . .

_____

_____

Love Life

- I intend . . .

_____

_____

- My action step is . . .

_____

_____

Career

- I intend . . .

_____

_____

- My action step is . . .

_____

_____

Religious or Spiritual Path

- I intend . . .

_____

_____

- My action step is . . .

_____

_____

FINAL THOUGHTS ON MANIFESTING ALL THAT YOU DESIRE

The routine I'm about to share with you has been a daily part of my life for many years now, and I know that by slowing down and adopting a similar program, you too can begin to live with more optimism, love, and energy.

Each morning when I get up, I go turn the coffeemaker on. Then, on the way back to my bedroom, I'll thank my plants for their beauty, thank God and my angels for another phenomenal day, and then lie back down for a 20- to 30-minute intention/gratitude meditation.

After a deep breath, I mentally open my mind, my eyes, nose, mouth, ears, throat, heart, soul, and body. For example, as I say "I open my mind," I envision the top of my head slowly opening up, and I repeat this for each part of my body. Then I take another deep breath and ask to be filled with God's patience, love, empathy, joy, abundance, grace, discipline, health, and spirit. From there I'll go into a session of gratitude where I'll give thanks for all that occurred the day before. I might be thankful for my sleep, the book I read, a delicious dinner, the friends I visited, the business I accomplished, my workout, the beauty of the day, or whatever, but I always try to specifically recall things to give thanks for. This period of gratitude slows me down and lets me relive the beauty of the previous day.

Next, I'll say an affirmation for each area of my life that I want to continue growing in and being blessed with. With each one, I ground myself by making the sign of the cross. Here are my affirmations:

- *Spirituality:* "I am healed and guided to a deeper sense of spirituality at this moment and every moment forward through God and my angels." I then see in my mind's eye my spiritual path becoming stronger.

- *Emotions:* "I am healed and guided to a deeper sense of emotional strength at this moment and every moment forward through God and my angels." I then see in my mind's eye my emotional state becoming stronger.

- *Physical health:* "I am healed and guided to a healthier state physically at this moment and every moment forward through God and my angels." I then see in my mind's eye my physical health becoming stronger.

- *Career path:* "I am healed and guided to a deeper connection with my career path at this moment and every moment forward through God and my angels." I then see in my mind's eye my career path being enhanced.

- *Financial wealth:* "I am healed and guided to more abundance financially at this moment and every moment forward through God and my angels." I then see in my mind's eye my financial wealth growing daily, of which I give 10 percent of my gross income to help others.

- *Love:* "I am healed and guided to a more loving state at this moment and every moment forward through God and my angels." I then see in my mind's eye my deep love of others as well as myself.

At the end of this session, I ask to be guided to reach my maximum potential in every area of my life. Then I arise, enjoy my coffee, and begin my day.

INTENTION INTO ACTION

Before I truly immersed myself in the concept of slowing down as often as possible during the entire day, my conscious decision to live life with intention and gratitude would end right here. But as I continued to look for new avenues that allowed me to slow down even more, I found that when I asked throughout the day to be more patient, loving, and aware, opportunities arose offering me the chance to do just that. Now I recommend to all my clients that they slow down, and before they leave their houses, mentally go through a list of intentions as they drive to work.

I remember a client named Monica whose daily intention meditation led to action and phenomenal results. She was an engineer at a large corporation, and she had just been given a great promotion. But her excitement was stymied on the day she walked into her first meeting to see 20 male engineers sitting in front of her with "Prove your competency to us" written across their faces. This was a challenge she wasn't prepared for. Their lack of support continued for weeks, and it became evident that they wanted her to feel like an outsider. (She later found out that there were several people in this group who had been passed over when she was selected for the promotion, and they were determined to make her life miserable at best.)

Although she was normally an extremely organized and competent person, during our first session together, Monica told me that she was becoming unglued. Her confidence was waning and she found herself uncharacteristically scattered, starting a variety of projects at work and at home but never completing them.

I asked Monica to slow down and evaluate all the possible sources of stress and struggle in her life at that moment. Then, together we created a series of intentions for her to repeat before she left her house each morning and once again before she got out of her car at work. I knew that if she continued to let her mind race, nothing would change, so I asked her to create the intention to become calmer, to listen to someone else's opinion before stating her own, and to have gratitude for everything that was going right in her life.

This practice immediately began to help Monica become centered. She felt a shift every time she slowed down and repeated her intentions, so instead of walking into work in a frenzied state worrying about all that could possibly go wrong that day, she calmly repeated them. She began walking more slowly and confidently from her car to her office, and she also began to take five minute breaks, two times a day, where she would again slow down and repeat the end result she desired to manifest into her life. Her intention and gratitude led to action, and she became a competent, goal-oriented, compassionate, centered, and strong leader. At our final session, she told me that without a doubt, the use of daily intentions was the key to her own internal turnaround.

Your intention might be as simple as smiling at everyone you see at work today. By mentally rehearsing this action before even arriving at the office, your daily thoughts turn into the action steps that improve your daily life.

✳

I personally can't imagine a better, more grounded way to begin my day than to be immersed in gratitude, intention, and action. This process is designed to slow us down, and it does. It's designed to help us become more optimistic and centered, which will lead us to more joy and peace.

At first, many of my clients will admit that they hesitated to add one more task to their daily schedule, but once they realized that all they had to start with was a simple mental exercise each morning, they agreed to give it a shot. And within a very short period of time, results began to show. That's because when you expect good things to happen, you put yourself in a position that's unstoppable. So do yourself a favor and make the commitment to go after what you desire.

Intention, gratitude, and action truly are the three keys to manifesting what you desire in your life, and this simple system will allow you to reach your maximum potential in just minutes a day. All you need to do is slow down and reap the many rewards that will come your way.

❀ ❀ ❀

Part I Review

Take a moment or two to slow down and review the information presented in the previous pages. Remember that the writing exercises are truly the hidden gems of this work, and your written answers at the end of each part of this book will help you focus, create the intention to change, and then propel you forward as you set your action plan into motion.

The act of writing allows you to delve deeper into your mind to recall from the previous pages the information that was important to *you* and relevant to *your* life and desires. I believe that this is one of the many powerful steps that you can take in order to create the life you desire. So slow down, think, write, and then become who you truly want to be.

Please answer the following questions:

1. What was covered, in detail, in this section?

_____

_____

_____

_____

2. What was of most interest to you, and why?

_____

_____

_____

_____

3. What's the current plan of action you'll institute to help you achieve your goal? (Specifically list the steps you'll take to live the life you really want to.)

_____

_____

_____

_____

When you slow down and incorporate intention, gratitude, and a plan of action into your life, you'll start to feel more at peace and certain of your path. In Part II, you'll build on the principles of slowing down by learning how to maximize your power in every area of life.

❋ ❋ ❋

PART II

Slow Down

to Maximize Your
Personal Power

chapter 4

Understanding the Power Within

The most successful people I know understand the importance of maximizing their personal power every day to create a life of abundance and joy, and they do this by living honestly and with integrity.

A number of years ago, I went to a lecture given by my good friend Joe Cirulli, who's revered around the world for his work in the fitness industry—in fact, Joe's health clubs in Gainesville have been ranked as some of the top facilities in the world. At this lecture, he was defining what he saw as the characteristics of a successful person. One of the attributes he mentioned, which has stuck with me ever since, was that successful people applaud the accomplishments of those around them. Whether the person is a friend, family member, or ex-spouse, successful people congratulate individuals when they accomplish their goals. They're so comfortable with themselves that they can look into the eyes of those who have achieved something worthwhile and recognize their efforts. They're full of personal power.

Still, many of us regularly give away our personal power to others by withholding our true feelings. Some of us have even watched relationships with close friends and lovers crumble because we're too afraid to let them know how we really feel. In fact, some people find it easier to give an inconsiderate stranger a piece of their mind than to tell someone close to them that they consider *their* actions thoughtless. And on the other side of the coin, we also diminish our power by *not* giving someone a compliment when they deserve it.

It should come as no surprise that the more we give our personal power away, the less respect we have for ourselves. And it's truly a vicious circle, because a loss of self-respect can only lead to one thing: diminished personal power.

I'm sure you can guess that there's only one way to win your personal power back and to begin living a life filled with more integrity, love, and happiness: Slow down, look deeply into the situations where you give your power away, and then ask yourself why you do so. Realize that you can change your current behavior and reclaim what's rightfully yours— confidence, integrity, and power—from this day forward.

In relationships, you may give your power away to others by not being honest with them about what you want out of the partnership. Maybe you don't want to rock the boat and let someone know that you don't agree with him or her. But by slowing down, you can admit to your past or current errors, correct them, and move on to a better place.

And what about how you act in your professional life? I've worked with clients who gave their power away to co-workers and bosses so many times that they ended up feeling unworthy of the greatness that truly resided within them. In accepting responsibility for mistakes that weren't theirs, taking consistent criticism despite work that was well done, and feeling that they weren't strong enough to stand up to injustice in the workplace, they all eventually suffered a lack of self-esteem and a diminished sense of personal power.

If you find yourself in the mind-set of "Who am I to stand up to the bullies of the world?" then it's time to step back and remember all the people before you who have reclaimed their power and gone on to feel free and full of energy. Maybe it's time to see the movie *Erin Brockovich*, which tells the story of one woman who took on the world to fight for justice. She was someone who, prior to deciding to slow down and reclaim her personal power, had let the opinions of others run her life. When she finally stood up for herself, she reclaimed her power and found a way to help those in need.

DON'T LET JEALOUSY DRAIN YOUR POWER

Have you ever given your power away to someone else because they have what you want? Have you ever been envious of another person's success? If so, do you realize that by holding on to your jealousy, you're actually giving your power away?

Jealousy, like anger, is simply an emotion—one to be acknowledged and dealt with, not submerged and ignored. In fact, it can actually be a good motivator. For example, if you're resentful of someone who has a great intimate relationship, you can take that energy and improve yourself in order to be a better lover. If you're envious of someone who has a lot of money, you can harness that feeling to maximize your skills in business. If you find yourself wishing you had someone else's beautiful body, then by all means, use that as an incentive to develop a workout and nutrition regime.

The bottom line is that when you hold on to your jealousy, you lose your personal power. When you express your emotion in writing, in conversation with a friend, or in a counseling session, you can release it—and maybe even use it to your advantage.

This reminds me of a young woman who called in to my radio show one day with a personal dilemma. She told me that her best friend had just been hired for a job that she'd coveted for years. This young woman was upset because she knew that this position had the potential to catapult her to future success, and she wanted to know if her jealousy was normal. She asked me how she could possibly congratulate her friend when deep inside she wanted the job for herself.

First, I asked the caller if this situation was one that she had any control over. Her answer was no. "So, are you willing to lose a friend over something that's out of your control?" I inquired. Again, she said no.

"What if the shoe was on the other foot?" I went on. "How would you feel if your best friend was upset with you and jealous that you beat her out of her dream job?"

"I'd feel that she was acting immature and self-centered," the caller admitted.

All of a sudden, it was as if a light went off in her head. "I get it," she said.

We went on to discuss the power she had within to take this initial jealousy and use it for her own good. My advice to her was to feel it, and then let it go by congratulating her friend for her success. Then she could look at the situation and see where her efforts needed to be focused to improve her chances the next time—or whether she needed to move in a completely different direction.

One time, a reporter from a local TV station called in to my radio show. She had just gone through a divorce when the station she worked for decided to add a new lifestyle show to their daily lineup. Since she'd been doing so well and anticipating advancement, she was particularly disturbed when her ex-husband, who had been a news reporter, got the job. She was heartbroken, angry, and jealous, and her emotional response started to negatively affect every part of her life. Her ex was the one in the limelight now, and she wasn't able to handle his success. She couldn't help but feel that this should have been *her* big break.

It's easy to see that she was giving her power away to him, and yet the new show went on without her. All she was doing was depleting her own energy. This type of situation is one that offers you a choice: You can move ahead and use a situation to enhance your own personal power, or you can let it tear you apart.

Have you been giving your power away by holding on to jealousy? Perhaps an ex-spouse or lover found a new partner and you're resentful of their happiness. Maybe your neighbor recently purchased a new car, which makes you feel "less" than he is. Or it could be that a co-worker was just given recognition that you feel should have been bestowed upon you. It might even be the case that your girlfriend's beautiful new engagement ring makes your blood boil with envy. I don't mean to suggest that it isn't normal to feel sadness, loss, anger, or jealousy in situations such as these, but if you hold on to those feelings for long, you'll lose your positive energy and stay mired in negativity.

You can regain your lost power by slowing down, feeling your emotions, writing them down, and letting them go. Do whatever it takes: Maybe consider working with a counselor or coach, but just don't let your emotions stay within. Take a moment now to answer the following questions.

- Whom do you feel envious of because they've achieved something that you desire?

_____

_____

- How can you use that energy to your advantage —to accomplish your goals?

_____

_____

Do you see how envy and jealousy can actually diminish your personal power? As Joe Cirulli said, you become more successful when you cheer when others succeed. I'd go so far as to say that your power can be enhanced even more if you celebrate the successes of those who have what you want. Slow down and release the feelings that are holding you back. Applaud someone else's victory, focus your energy on going after your own goals, and then you'll reclaim your power.

FINDING YOUR OWN PATH TO PERSONAL POWER

You may be wondering if there are any other ways to work toward letting go of your envy. You may be thinking, _Do I really have to applaud my competitor? Could I ever congratulate an ex-partner who treated me unkindly, or an ex-boss who was unfair?_ These are questions only you can answer, but I will say that I've never met a truly happy and successful person who hasn't found a healthy way to release jealousy. Your energy levels could be depleted for years if you don't move past these upsets and disappointments. That doesn't mean that it's always an easy thing to do, or that it will happen overnight, but do you really have any other options if your goal is to restore your personal power?

If you give your power away to someone who hurt you, or to someone you're jealous of, then you'll never be able to get all that you truly want out of life. Slow down, go within, and find *your* path.

If you need to, use this exercise to imagine how you'll feel when you regain your power.

- How would you feel today if you were able to let go of your jealousy or resentment of certain people in your life (ex-partners, bosses, family members, neighbors, friends, and so on)? Write, in detail, what it would feel like to let go of that burden.

_____

_____

_____

_____

_____

_____

chapter 5

Increase Your Power in Every Area of Your Life

The saying "The older I get, the less I know" is funny and true. Regardless of how old we are or how much we think we've learned, we're still simply students in this dance called life. Sometimes it may seem like a humbling experience to ask for help—perhaps because we're supposed to be "experts" at something, or because we've reached a certain age. But we all need to keep in mind that asking for help is a sign of strength, not weakness. It actually takes a very strong person to admit that they need help with an addiction, a floundering relationship, a stalled career, or any other challenging situation—and the individual with a strong sense of personal power knows that requesting assistance is a logical step to future success.

BE WILLING TO ASK FOR WHAT YOU WANT

In their book *The Aladdin Factor,* authors Mark Victor Hansen and Jack Canfield share the story of a married couple who always went to the same camp in the woods for rest and relaxation. As most couples do, they had each assumed certain responsibilities in preparing for their vacation. Upon arriving, the wife would walk down the many stairs to the cottage to get the kitchen ready to store the food they brought for their stay, and her husband would begin his numerous trips to unload the groceries from the car.

On one occasion, after he'd emptied the car, the man sat in the kitchen with a disgruntled look on his face. When his wife asked him what was wrong, he blurted out, "You know, for ten years you've never once helped me bring the groceries down that long flight of stairs." His wife replied, "I'm sorry, honey, but you never asked me to help you. How was I to know you really needed my help without your asking for it?"

I had firsthand experience with asking for what I needed when I was working on my second children's book, *Papa's Amazing Tales: Diamond the Dolphin.* I had chosen to self-publish, and I'd invested a lot of time and money into the project. I knew that I needed an excellent illustrator, but couldn't afford to pay someone up front for the job. As luck would have it, I ran into a young artist named Barbra Doctor who loved the idea of becoming a part of my second book. So, without hesitation, I asked her to create the illustrations for a percentage of the royalties once the book was published. Barbra agreed, and the project became a wonderful success.

My own sense of power continues to grow every time I ask for what I desire. And when the answer is no, I pick up and move on, knowing that something better awaits me ahead. Of course that's not always easy to do, but I know I can't lose by asking for what I want. Even if the answer is no, I tell myself that I might have just been saved from a situation that wouldn't have worked out anyway. That's the attitude of an individual with personal power.

So what do you really want? A raise or a promotion, a date with someone you're attracted to, help in changing the shape of your body, or the money to pursue a lifelong dream? You'll probably be surprised to see how far you can get in life just by making a simple request. As it was so plainly stated in the Bible, "Ask, and you shall receive."

It's rare that what you want will just walk up and drop itself in your lap, so slow down and complete the next exercise to get clear on what it is that you truly desire.

- What do you long for that you don't have in your life right now (love, health, wealth, inner peace, freedom from bad habits)?

- Now that you know what you want, who can help you get it? (You can list more than one person or organization.)

- Write down the exact date and time that you'll contact these people/organizations.

Now, to build your inner power, follow through and contact those who can help you get what you want. Many people are surprised to discover how willing others are to give assistance, because they never asked. Reach out and watch your success grow.

RECLAIM YOUR POWER BY RELEASING THOSE WHO HAVE HURT YOU

I've often wondered why we give our power away to those who have hurt us by trying to understand *why* they acted the way they did. Aren't we just setting ourselves up for frustration when we constantly try to understand the motive behind their actions? Isn't there a better use of our energy than fretting over a past experience—one that's out of our control?

Over the years, many people called my radio show because they were still trying to find the answers to the following questions:

- Why did she leave me?

- Why did he take my money?

- Why did she lie to me?

- Why won't he talk to me?

- Why did she fire me?

- Why did he gossip about me?

- Why did she abuse me?

It's true that coming to some sort of closure with a past relationship may help you heal, but what if the other person won't communicate honestly with you, or they refuse to talk to you at all? Perhaps they were hurt by childhood experiences, or they have an ego that's gotten out of control. It could be that they're driven by greed, lust, or another emotion, or maybe they're facing a challenging situation. Their behavior could be about their need for control, their desire for power, or their lack of self-esteem (as we all know, those who like themselves least will often put others down in order to feel bigger). Whatever the case may be, sometimes you just have to accept that the reason they hurt you may never surface.

After the initial sting of a tough personal situation, most of us want some closure. But if the other party can't or won't work with you, how long should you sit around and ponder their motivation? Even if it's difficult, you should try to move forward, because by staying stuck in whys and hows, you just continue to give your power to the past.

Slow down for a minute and evaluate your own experience. Do you still have people in your life whom you're giving your power and energy away to for something they did to you months or years ago? Take a moment now and list these individuals. (If the thought of doing so brings up deep emotional pain, consider seeing a therapist who specializes in this area.)

- Individuals who have deeply hurt me, past or present:

_____

_____

_____

It's important to realize that we may never fully know the reasons for someone else's actions. And unless the people who have hurt us do the inner work necessary, they may never know the exact cause of their behavior either. On the other hand, even though an ex-partner may refuse to acknowledge his or her role in the disintegration of the union, years later it may be easier to admit mistakes. In fact, this recently happened to me.

One day, out of the blue, I received an e-mail from a woman I'd once pursued a relationship with. She told me that she wanted to express her sorrow for letting me down. She went on to accept full responsibility for her actions, and then called me to let me know that it was her issues that kept us apart. She said that while she couldn't admit to it at the time, it was important that I now know how sorry she was.

It was a wonderful gesture, but not everyone has the strength and awareness that this woman has. As I see it, that leaves you with two options: You can continue to use your energy to try to figure out someone else's behavior, or you can slow down and begin to move forward to regain your personal power. And of course, moving forward may mean releasing your need for closure.

Releasing past hurts is easier said than done, but answering the following questions may help you through the process:

- How can you grow from this experience? And what life lessons have you learned from this? (For example, you may see the need to slow down in future relationships, or to get to know people better before you commit your heart, time, and/or money to them.)

_____

_____

_____

- How can this experience make you a better person?

_____

_____

_____

- Have you, in the past or more recently, mis-treated anyone? (This is a question most of us want to say no to, but do yourself a favor—slow down and evaluate your actions. You may be surprised to see that you have hurt others in the same way you've been hurt.)

_____

_____

_____

- How can you prevent this experience from being repeated in the future?

When we accept our responsibility for staying in a relationship that has faded, we enhance our sense of self. My client Linda learned this when she decided to reclaim her personal power after a painful breakup. Here's what she had to say to me after one of our sessions:

> *You gave me new insight as to how to move on. I should have listened to my inner voice when it was telling me things were not as they should be. Now I realize that I need to accept some of the responsibility, not to just lament the fact that he left me. Maybe I should have been the one leaving long before. Having that knowledge—instead just thinking "Poor me, he left"—seems to help.*

Decide today to do the work necessary to let these past or present situations and people go. Take your newfound energy to help yourself heal, grow, and set an example for others as someone who truly has personal power. Then, through your words and actions, inspire others to do the same.

GIVING YOUR POWER AWAY BY
PUTTING OTHERS ABOVE YOURSELF

Are there people at work, school, or in your neighborhood that you put above you—that is, you give your power away to them by thinking they're so much better than you are? Would you back down from a discussion with a person who has a Ph.D. or an M.D. because you think, *Surely she must be smarter than I am?* Do you sheepishly walk past the man in the gym who has a "perfect" body? Do you ogle celebrities and wish you could just get close enough for a photo? If so, have you ever slowed down enough to see that every time you put other people on a pedestal, you're giving away your power?

When you let self-limiting thoughts such as *She's so much smarter . . . he's more creative . . . they're wealthier, prettier, and more talented than I am* run through your head, you stop looking at developing your own beauty and stay stuck in the "I'm not worthy" zone of life. And as you do this month after month and year after year, your sense of individuality becomes eroded.

Can you admire others and still keep your personal power? Of course you can. Practice it in your mind—appreciate those around you for their talent, beauty, knowledge, or whatever, but in a way that doesn't make you feel less important than they are. Avoid the "They're up there, I'm down here" mode of thinking. As I said in Chapter 4, applaud others' successes, but retain your power.

For example, imagine yourself standing next to a movie star you really admire. If you were idolizing her, you might say, "Oh my God—I can't believe it's you! I don't know what to say!" But if you looked at that same actor with appreciation *and* equality, you might respond like this: "It's so nice to meet you, Jane. I really admire the work you did in your latest movie."

In other words, let people know that they're special in your eyes, but don't forget that *you're* special, too. Little by little, these human beings who are full of their own issues and challenges become less intimidating every time you see them at work, on TV, or at the gym.

There have been times when I've been caught in the game of elevating certain people above myself, but gradually, this lesson is sinking in. Because of my radio and TV shows, I've had the chance to interview some high-profile celebrities, athletes, authors, and spiritual leaders over the years, and in the beginning, I was in total awe. I started to give my power away, and as I did, I felt worse about myself.

Several counselors I worked with, including intuitive counselor CJ Moon, told me of the potential problems I could face in my work in the media—one of which was to put celebrities on such a pedestal that I'd lose myself in the process. They warned me that if I did this, my interviews could begin to sound canned, almost contrived, as if I were just another fan. Since I was interviewing famous people every week, there was also the possibility that I might begin to see myself as superior to others.

Well, during one interview with an extremely successful author, I began to see that there was no need to put anyone above anyone else. I was broadcasting out of my home in Florida while my producer, Greg Bell, was in the main studio in Virginia. Shortly before we went on the air, Greg called the guest to let him know that he'd be on in a few minutes, and as always, asked if he'd like to hear the opening of my show to get a feel for what the program was about. The guest shot back with anger about how this interview was interrupting his day, and told Greg not to call him again until we were ready to start the interview. Greg, being a wonderfully sensitive soul, was hurt by the blatant attack by this man, who we'd both put way above us.

Greg didn't have time to tell me what was going on, so we proceeded with the interview, which, ironically, was about healing, emotions, and intimacy. During the first break, while the guest was on hold, Greg finally told me the story. I was so mad that he'd been treated this way that we cut the interview short.

Of course, I had hundreds of exceptional interviews with very successful people who were just angels to me and everyone else who worked on the show, but as you can imagine, this wasn't the only time an incident of this nature happened to Greg or some of my other producers. I'm grateful, though, because this situation taught me an important lesson: We need to be able to respect the success of others, but not give our power away to them. Ever since that interview, regardless of how big a celebrity a person might be, I have no interest in interviewing them if they treat people rudely.

Slow down and pay attention to whom you give your power away to—especially those people who you believe are above you in any of the ways mentioned—and begin today to see them in a new light. Be appreciative of their talents while keeping your own sense of self.

RECLAIM YOUR POWER BY STAYING TRUE TO WHO YOU ARE

Sometimes we're untrue to ourselves because we want to fit in and be liked by others. Maybe we don't want to stand up for our beliefs because we fear being judged, so we act one way with one group of friends and another way when circumstances change.

As challenging as it might be, the only way to feel really good about ourselves and enhance our personal power is to be true to who we are at all times. For many of us who feel the pressure of a society that says we need to be liked by all people at all times, this can be a daunting challenge. But by slowing down, we can leave the old behavior behind and relish our newfound power.

Time and again, people called my radio show for advice on maintaining their sense of self when they'd been conditioned since birth to be "nice," instead of to be themselves. And while I never told anyone to be rude, I did suggest that they discover their true values and live them daily.

Mahatma Gandhi often spoke about the need to stay true to one's self, regardless of what anyone else thinks. And on top of that, he asked people to be open to the fact that their truths may change from time to time. Those with a strong sense of self realize this, and aren't afraid to say, "Yes, I believed that before with all of my heart, but now I've found a different path." Like Republicans who become Democrats or Christians who become Jews, they need to be strong enough to stand up for what they know to be true at this moment. As Gandhi said so well: "At the time of writing I never think of what I have said before. My aim is not to be consistent with my previous statements on a given question, but to be consistent with truth as it may present itself to me at a given moment. The result has been that I have grown from truth to truth . . . "[1] That's personal power.

Slow down and examine your life to see if you're acting in ways that are true to what you believe. Have you ever found yourself changing your tune, depending on who you're talking to? Do you value being consistent more than

---

[1] *The Words of Gandhi*, selected by Richard Attenborough. (New York, NY: Newmarket Press, 1982)

being truthful? Can you see how this could actually strip away your personal power?

Perhaps you're married, and you used to believe that the "right" thing to do is stay married, even if the relationship is unsalvageable. If you've done all you can to work things out, yet being together isn't healthy for either party, would you stay consistent with your old belief, or would you be true to who you are as a person and separate or dissolve the union?

What about your career? If you've outgrown it, or you've simply lost interest in your field, do you keep going to work day after day, to a job that's not helping you fulfill your dreams? Or do you follow what you know to be true and begin looking for another career path that will inspire you and allow you to tap in to your full potential? Once you realize how important it is to respect and honor your changing truths, you'll know what to do.

I remember a number of years ago when I was criticized on my radio show for my discussion of the teachings of Buddha. I received several brutal e-mails and felt hurt inside, wondering how people could attack me so viciously when my intent was simply to share the benefits of different belief systems. I called my father, a devout Roman Catholic, to see what his thoughts were.

I was surprised to hear my dad say that his beliefs had changed quite drastically over the past 50 years. He admitted that when he was younger, he didn't believe anyone other than Roman Catholics could ever get into heaven. But as he gained knowledge and experience, what he believed to be true changed as well.

A powerful shift had occurred within my dad over the years—he'd followed his heart, rather than sticking with what he'd always believed just to be consistent. Dad said that he'd never leave his faith and that he knew being Catholic was the only path for him, but at the same time, he'd come to appreciate the fact that someone else could have a different set of beliefs. He stayed true to himself, even when his own set of truths changed radically over the years. He kept his personal power.

In my personal relationships and in my work in the media, I try to stay focused on what I know to be true today. At the same time, I look back on how I've changed over the years, and I try to be open to the fact that what I hold to be true for me at this moment regarding love, politics, health, or my career may continue to evolve.

LIVE WITH HONESTY

Almost all of us have given away our personal power at some time or another because we were afraid to be honest with ourselves or those around us. In fact, I'll bet it happens much more regularly than any of us wants to admit—just think about how many times you may have told a white lie or agreed with someone just to avoid rocking the boat!

Sometimes it's easier not to tell others how you truly feel, because it might reveal your vulnerability. But to keep your personal power, you need to leave the opinions of others behind and live the most honest life you can. There's no reason to be disrespectful to anyone who may harshly judge an experience you've had, but there's nothing to be gained by feeling ashamed of something you've gone through in life either.

Most people have an initial reaction to an event, and then they go on with their lives. After all, do you sit around thinking about all the mistakes your family, friends, and co-workers have made in the past? Would it really make a difference to you if you found out that a good friend is experiencing marital troubles or used to have a drug addiction? Remembering this may help you let go of your own shame and guilt.

Being honest with yourself and others isn't always the simplest path, but it's the only one to take if you want to enhance your personal power. It's time to slow down and live honestly.

You Hold the Key to Unlocking Your Personal Power

"What you connect with, you already know." This maxim is so important to the process of living a powerful life. You see, we're all so much smarter than we give ourselves credit for, but when we're under stress, our knowledge and intuition can get "covered up." So we seek out coaches, counselors, or other "experts" to help us find answers, and then sit in awe when they make a statement that resonates with us.

Well, take it from me, it's always easier when you're sitting on the outside, looking in. If I happen to say something that helps a client see her challenge in a new way, I'm not the one with all the knowledge—she is. My client couldn't have connected with my statement so wholeheartedly if she didn't already know it to be true. In my very first session with every new client, I make sure that they understand the truth of this philosophy: What we connect with so quickly when said by another person, we already know to be true.

Think about something another person has said that you agree with on the deepest level. Whatever it was, you already knew it to be true. Now, it may have been something you learned in childhood and simply forgot. Sometimes information simply gets buried in your subconscious, until one day when you're listening to an audiotape with quotes from the Dalai Lama or Margaret Thatcher, and you get an "Aha" to a life question you have. Right after you mentally give the author of the quote kudos for being so eloquent, slow down and congratulate *yourself*. For you can't agree with something if you didn't already know it to be true—period.

I want you to work on this most critical component of personal growth daily. Begin building a solid base of personal power by realizing how incredibly intelligent you are today.

A FINAL LOOK AT YOUR PERSONAL POWER

Here are a few of the most notable ways to reclaim your personal power:

1. Release your need to be liked and accepted by others.

2. Take time away from a job or relationship that has hit a wall, even if it means you may lose that position or person.

3. Express how you feel soon after an event has occurred, instead of submerging your emotions for weeks, months, or longer.

4. Honestly admit your mistakes as soon as possible.

5. Laugh at your humanness.

6. Congratulate those who have accomplished their goals.

7. Walk away from a person or job that's controlling you or draining you of your personal power.

I know that the personal power you desire is closer for you to experience than you may realize at this very moment, but it can't be obtained without slowing down to see all that you currently have, as well as the changes that need to be made. At this very moment, you have everything you need to live a strong, happy, and real life. It's up to you to start believing this truth.

❋ ❋ ❋

Part II Review

Take a moment or two to slow down and review the information presented in Part II. Remember that the writing exercises are truly the hidden gems of this work, and your written answers at the end of each part of this book will help you focus, create the intention to change, and then propel you forward as you set your action plan into motion.

The act of writing allows you to delve deeper into your mind to recall from the previous pages the information that was important to *you* and relevant to *your* life and desires. I believe that this is one of the many powerful steps that you can take in order to create the life you desire. So slow down, think, write, and then become who you truly want to be.

Please answer the following questions:

1. What was covered, in detail, in this section?

_____

_____

_____

_____

2. What was of most interest to you, and why?

_____

_____

_____

3. What's the current plan of action you'll institute to help you achieve your goal? (Specifically list the steps you'll take to live the life you really want to.)

_____

_____

_____

_____

Maximizing your personal power can lead to great accomplishments both personally and professionally. Now move on to Part III, where you'll discover how to use the principles of slowing down in order to get the body, energy, and health you've always wanted.

❋ ❋ ❋

PART III

Slow Down

to Get the Body,

Energy, and Health

You've Always Wanted

chapter 6

Get the Body You've Always Wanted: An Exercise Program for Everyone

This chapter is about creating the body you've always wanted, finding ways to enhance your energy level, and getting healthier at the same time. As you've probably already guessed, the only way to do all this is by slowing down enough to examine how you're living your life today and exploring the changes you need to make so that you can truly get what you want.

I'll admit up front that some of the information in this chapter might surprise you, and some of the steps I'll ask you to consider taking to transform your body may seem strange. But I'll back up my claims and recommendations with stories that prove how effective this system really is.

My programs to enhance health and physique were first devised in the 1980s, during my graduate work as I pursued my master's degree in fitness management. Following this, I created a series of popular exercise videos that incorporated both strength and aerobic exercise with companies such as The Step and SPRI, the makers of exercise equipment including rubber resistance bands and tubing. The final touches to the program that you'll read about in this book were added through my radio interviews and meetings with some of the top experts and authors in diet and exercise from around the country.

So slow down, and get ready to throw out some of your long-held beliefs about health and fitness. By doing these two things, you'll finally be ready to get the body, energy, and health you've always wanted.

TRANSFORM YOUR PHYSIQUE THROUGH STRENGTH TRAINING

During the last year of my national radio show, I received many calls from people asking if the "body transformation" contests that everyone was talking about really worked. In many fitness magazines, companies were showing before-and-after photos of seemingly out-of-shape people who, in just 12 weeks, had transformed their bodies into sculpted works of art. Of course, these contests were being used as advertising to sell nutritional products, so the companies only showed the elite participants from the program—those who were genetically gifted or had been training hard for years and just needed to lose body fat. But what I loved most about these advertisements was that they made people slow down and wonder *Can I really change my body in such a dramatic fashion?* The answer I gave to them is *yes!*

You may not become a fitness cover model if you follow the recommendations set forth here, but you *can* transform how you look if you radically change your approach to exercise. That doesn't necessarily mean hours and hours in the gym, but it does mean working smarter. And the key to any body transformation is *strength training*.

Many people, especially women, initially balk at the notion that strength training has anything to do with helping them get the body they've always wanted. They erroneously buy into the notion that aerobics, walking, and running hold the magical key to achieving their physical goals. While aerobic training is wonderful and helpful, strength training is what makes the difference between an average physique and a great one. (And ladies, please don't be afraid of gaining huge muscle mass through strength training. Due to lower testosterone levels and smaller muscle fibers, 97 percent of women couldn't get large muscles unless they took anabolic steroids, so let that fear go.)

The thing is that when you strength-train, you increase lean muscle tissue, which burns more calories than fat does when the body is at rest. So the more of this lean tissue you have, the more calories you'll burn 24 hours a day—even when you're not working out. In fact, studies have shown that the body continues to burn an increased amount of calories for up to ten hours after a 30-minute strength-training session, which is just one of the many reasons why total-body strength training is a must for people of all ages who truly want to see their figure transformed in front of their eyes.

I remember interviewing Cory Everson, a six-time Ms. Olympia bodybuilding champion, about the amount of time it takes to achieve the body one desires with strength training. She told me that when she was competing, contestants all held on to the false belief that building a powerful physique demanded four to six hours a day in the gym. But today, with all the recent advancements in scientific studies in regards to strength training, Cory said she needs no more than 45 minutes, four days a week, to look and feel fantastic. And does she ever look great! Cory practices what she preaches, and her results are phenomenal. She's a true beauty inside and out.

A woman named Rebecca came to me in the early '90s for workout advice. She was burned out on her old "aerobics only" workouts because she never got the results she desired. She was ready to really apply herself in a new way, so we added a sound strength-training program to her routine. Within a few months, the transformation had begun.

The first place I noticed a change was in Rebecca's legs. They were already in good condition due to her daily runs, but now they were sleek, strong, and—yes—sexy. I remember her coming to a session once, laughing about all the compliments she was getting. Years of running hadn't given her the phenomenal legs that she had sculpted in just a few months of strength training.

By the third month, I could see some wonderful changes occurring in Rebecca's upper body as well, particularly in her shoulders and back. But what occurred physically is only half of the story. After seeing how much healthier and sexier she looked, she decided to use her success to help those who wanted to improve their body. Rebecca became a personal trainer so that she could share the exciting transformation she'd experienced firsthand with others.

Since I was recently divorced and ready for some positive change, I decided to get in shape—physically and mentally. I'd been active most of my life, and for years I'd been jogging, biking, and doing aerobics at the gym, so I was surprised that my first serious attempt at strength training truly transformed my 35-year-old body and my life. Not only did my body respond, but emotionally I felt stronger than ever, too. Throughout this transformation, I looked the best I ever had, I was happier, and my life was more in balance. I then changed careers and became a certified personal trainer. I went back to school,

*got my degree in psychology, and have continued to train
people and stay fit for the last ten years.*

The most incredible thing about strength training is that
it changes you in more ways than you could ever imagine.
While the physical changes are to be expected, so many of
the other benefits, such as the ones described here, are
completely unexpected. Rebecca not only gained a new
awareness of her physical and emotional potential, but created a new career path as well. And all of this began with a
simple and effective strength-training program. If you slow
down, the same can happen to you.

More often than not, people who are against weight
training before they begin a program become evangelists for
this activity once they see how dramatically their bodies
change. If I could make one plea to people who want a
slim, slender, or sexy body, it would be to make strength
training an important priority in their lives. Open your
mind to the potential that the body you desire *is* achievable.

As an aside, while many women stay focused on their
legs, hips, and buttocks, really balanced and beautiful
physiques are achieved by working the upper body as well.
Women with defined upper bodies look fantastic and carry
themselves with more confidence, which allows them to
make healthier decisions in every area of their lives. And of
course, when you only work the lower half of your body, you
miss the opportunity of having the musculature of the entire
body assisting you in burning more calories at rest. (Remember, the more lean tissue you have, the more calories you
burn at rest; the more calories you burn at rest, the less fat
you'll have on your body; and the less fat you have, the
better you'll look and feel.)

MAKING TIME FOR EXERCISE

Now is the perfect time to let go of any old beliefs that support the fact that you don't have time to exercise. Nonsense! You don't have any legitimate reason not to, and the longer you hold on to this erroneous belief, the longer it will be before you get the body you've always wanted—if you ever do. Strong words? Maybe, but ones that are full of truth.

When it comes to the excuse "I don't have time to strength-train," I have one response: You need less time than you think to begin the physical transformation process. Study after study has proven that just one set of 6 to 12 repetitions per body part, two to three days a week, can yield fantastic results—for those who are new to exercise as well as fitness veterans. For most of us, this might add up to 20 to 25 minutes of strength training three days a week. In addition, I believe that doing some aerobic training is extremely beneficial, especially for reducing stress and enhancing the overall functioning of the cardiovascular system (most experts recommend 30 to 45 minutes of aerobic training three days per week).

How you choose to fit this in to your daily schedule is totally up to you. You can exercise three days a week and do both your aerobic and strength training together on the same days, or you can split them up and work out six days a week. I recommend that you choose a routine that fits your current lifestyle. The important thing to remember here is that to achieve anything great in life, you must slow down and make it a priority.

Once you start, you may find that regular exercise actually gives you *more* time because it can improve the quality of sleep you get. Many people who begin an exercise program find themselves sleeping soundly through the night and waking up in the morning with more energy than they've ever had.

If you're serious about your desires, you'll see that you *can* find the time necessary to create and sculpt the body you really want. And think about how you'll feel when you're proud of the body you have! So drop the excuses . . . now!

ACCOMPLISHING MORE IN LESS TIME

Until I started training with Joe Cirulli, owner of the renowned Gainesville Health & Fitness Center, I really didn't have much faith in the type of strength training I just outlined. Doing just one set of 6 to 12 repetitions didn't seem like it could be enough work to totally change your body. I'd always believed (regardless of how many studies I read that supported Joe's way of training) that doing multiple sets was the only way to change body shape and increase the strength of each muscle. Boy, was I wrong. After doing just one set of chest exercises the first day I worked out with Joe, I was a believer: The key to transforming the body is intense, brief workouts.

After my second session with Joe, where we exercised my legs, my thighs were shaking after only one set. I was amazed at how incredibly effective this method of training is. So if you're a person with little time to exercise but you still want wonderful results, this system is for you.

One of the keys to this type of workout is to use a slow count for each repetition, allowing more of each muscle to work through each movement. As more of the muscle is allowed to contract, the entire muscle is forced to get stronger. When you use fast movements for each repetition, momentum comes into play, which allows you to use more weight. But you're not really working the muscle fibers as effectively as you do when you practice slow reps.

When you're doing slow reps for the first time, concentrate on counting slowly from one to four for a single repetition, hesitating at the halfway point, and then using the same counting system to lower the weight back to the starting position. This technique is slow, controlled, and effective. Joe highly recommends using a 20-second approach to each repetition, where you count slowly from one to ten, hesitate, and then repeat the same counting method on your return to the starting position. This is the way we'd train together weekly, and I still follow this plan today. (For a more detailed description of a variety of actual workout plans, check out Joyce L. Vedral's book *Weight Training Made Easy*, or *Body for Life* by Bill Phillips.)

I'd love to share some stories Joe told me to prove that this type of training is great for even the most conditioned athletes. Joe received a call one day from a professional sprinter, who wanted to train at Joe's club while he was in town. As they talked, Joe mentioned that he'd be available to take the man through a workout if he was interested. Upon arriving at the facility, Joe explained his theory of one-set training, to which the sprinter replied that he'd rather stick with his own method. Finally, after a few minutes of Joe explaining why this was the best way to train, the man agreed to try it, but said that if after the first muscle group he didn't feel the system was working, he'd go his own way.

Joe chose the leg press as the first exercise. If you'd have seen the sprinter's thighs, which are the size of redwood trees, you'd wonder why Joe didn't go for a smaller muscle first. But Joe knew the power behind exercising for brief but intense periods of time. After doing four reps at 20 seconds each on the leg press, the skeptical sprinter proceeded to get off of the machine, take three steps, and almost fall to the ground. His legs were so exhausted from doing one set of slow and controlled reps that they nearly buckled! The track star was amazed—Joe Cirulli wasn't at all.

Another time, Joe was explaining the benefits of a particular line of exercise machines to a group of physical therapists, and he mentioned his belief in the one-set system of training. One of the therapists, a former Marine, just couldn't believe that this type of training was effective at all. And while he respected Joe's knowledge and reputation in this industry, he insisted that he needed multiple sets for every muscle group to experience an effective workout. Well, after one brief session with Joe, his opinion was changed forever.

❋

Sometimes we need to stretch our minds and try new methods of training to get the body we desire. I know because this happened to me, and it just might happen to you. I didn't think that Joe Cirulli's training would work for me at first, but it did. In fact, after just eight months, I saw wonderful results. Recently I ran into a woman I hadn't seen in eight years, all she wanted to talk about was transforming her body like I had done. It was flattering and fun at the same time, and I know that if you slow down and give this technique a chance, you too can get the body you've always wanted.

FINDING A PROGRAM YOU'LL STICK WITH

Even though I believe in my heart and soul that strength training should be a part of *everyone's* exercise routine, let me share a story about someone who took a different route to achieve the body she desired. A few years ago, I received an e-mail from a listener detailing the success story of a friend of hers who also listened to my national radio show, but who was too shy to write me. For years, the shy one had tried all kinds of diets in an attempt to lose the extra 100 pounds she was carrying around, but nothing worked.

This woman had heard me say that exercise is even more important than diet in helping people get closer to their ideal body weight. I felt then, and still do today, that if people would just forget about dieting and get into the habit of daily exercise, they'd have a much better chance of achieving their fitness goals than by dieting alone or trying to diet and add exercise at the same time. (After they've added a regular exercise program to their daily life, then they can wholeheartedly revamp their diet.)

Numerous times on my radio show, I'd talked about the need to start slow. I told my listeners to begin by walking, and after a month or two, intersperse short jogs with longer periods of walking to condition the body, so that eventually it would be able to handle the stress of running. Then, they could simply increase the pace and distance at a comfortable rate. (While this is by no means the only type of fitness program I endorse, for many people, walking—whether outdoors or on a treadmill—is one of the easiest programs to get started with.)

Initially, the shy woman wasn't convinced that this routine could actually help her achieve her goal, but she began to walk. (As I said before, many of us, including myself, need to slow down and try something that at first we don't think will work.) Every day, she'd simply put one foot in front of the other and head out the door. Within a short period of time, she was feeling so good about herself that she began to do a little jogging. As she saw her body slowly changing, she started to jog for longer periods of time during her walks, until eventually she was jogging several miles each day.

A year later, this woman reached her goal of losing 100 pounds, and according to her friend, it changed her life in every way imaginable—from how she looked to how she felt about herself. And it all began because she was able to slow down and do what she didn't think she could.

THE POWER OF YOGA

While you've probably heard of people who have transformed their body through aerobic exercise and/or strength training, would you believe that it's possible to make a major change in your physique with yoga? Years ago, my answer to this question would have been no. Even though I'm a huge fan of yoga because of the benefits it offers in the areas of stress reduction, flexibility, and spirituality, I never knew that this activity could help you become more muscularly defined, and I wouldn't have recommended it as part of a fitness routine—that is, until I met a man who slowed down, took a friend's advice to try yoga, and reaped the benefits he was looking for.

I met television producer Carl Lauten during the filming of an infomercial I cohosted in the early '90s. As the "fitness expert" of the show, I was asked for my opinion about what it truly takes to reshape one's body by several people on the set. Well, one day it was Carl who shared how yoga had changed his body and his life.

Carl had tried every type of exercise program available to reshape his body. Personal trainers had recommended all types of diets and routines to him, but none worked. A friend suggested that Carl try yoga, so he decided to commit himself to taking a class five days a week for six months. At the end of this period of time, much to his surprise and satisfaction, he'd achieved the change in his body that no other program had given him. He also noticed a difference in how he handled stress, as well as an increase in his spiritual and creative approach to life. Carl slowed down, challenged his own beliefs, and came out the victor.

While I have yet to see any scientific studies that prove yoga as a powerful program for weight loss or building muscle mass, I believe that one of the reasons it works has to do with its ability to help us release stress, leading to a more balanced emotional life. And the more balanced we are, the less emotional eating we'll do. Also, because yoga utilizes all of the muscles in the body in each workout, there could be an increase in lean muscle tissue, which, as I said before, means that the body will burn more calories 24 hours a day.

For whatever reason, yoga worked for Carl, and it could be just the right form of exercise to help you get and keep the body you've always wanted. But this will only happen if you slow down and do something different from what you're doing right now.

CHARTING YOUR SUCCESS

Exercise journals are powerful tools that can help you get focused on your goals and most important, stick with your plan. Your journal can be as simple or as detailed as you want it to be. (As with most other life-changing tools, I don't believe that there's a right or wrong way to create and use a journal.) The most important thing is to find or create a method that you connect with and then chart your progress weekly.

A simplified journal may look like this:

Day of the Week	Aerobic Exercise: No. of Minutes	Strength Exercise (Muscles Worked)
Monday	Walk: 45 min.	Chest, shoulders, triceps
Tuesday	—	—
Wednesday	Walk/jog: 45 min.	Back, biceps, abdominals
Thursday	—	—
Friday	Stationary bike: 15 min./ walk: 15 min.	Legs and lower back
Saturday	Yoga class: 45 min.	Back, biceps, abdominals
Sunday	—	—

You can use the following blank journal template to set your goals for the next week. Fill in the blanks with what you plan to do during each of the next seven days.

Day of the Week	Aerobic Exercise: No. of Minutes	Strength Exercise (Muscles Worked)
Monday		
Tuesday		
Wednesday		
Thursday		
Friday		
Saturday		
Sunday		

Now, in the following chart, record what you actually accomplished to see how close you came to matching the goals you set in the previous chart.

Day of the Week	Aerobic Exercise: No. of Minutes	Strength Exercise (Muscles Worked)
Monday		
Tuesday		
Wednesday		
Thursday		
Friday		
Saturday		
Sunday		

By using this type of journal chart each week, you can track your success and compare what you actually achieve to the goals you set. In fact, the simple act of writing down your goals can help you be more accountable. You can talk all you want about how this is the week that you'll begin or change your exercise program, but unless it's written down, it's easy to avoid following through with your good intentions.

Take a moment to record your goals, and later, write down what you actually accomplished. When you slow down and use an exercise journal, you'll be taking the first step toward making your fitness dreams a reality.

❅ ❅ ❅

chapter 7

Dietary Changes That Will Transform Your Body

Just as you have to challenge conventional wisdom about the type of exercise you should do to get the body you want, you need to examine old beliefs with respect to the eating habits and dietary practices you've adopted over the years. You must understand that if the way you're eating isn't giving you the body you want, you're going to have to try a new system. (See your doctor before making any changes in your diet, especially if you have health problems, including any type of kidney disorder.)

I've spoken to many fitness experts (and novices) over the years and have heard the same thing repeatedly: Once you have your body in great physical shape, your diet can have a bigger effect on how you look than the type of exercise program you do. That sounds amazing, doesn't it? But I've seen this proven time and again—both in my own life and in the lives of my clients. As I said in the previous chapter, to get the body you've always wanted, you have to exercise regularly. But once you've established a fitness routine, the fastest way to transforming your body is to seriously refine the way you eat.

THE HIGH-PROTEIN DIET

Back in the early '90s, a former girlfriend tried to convince me of the benefits of a high-protein diet. I'd been a fan of the high-carbohydrate diet for years, and didn't believe that changing what I ate could actually improve my body shape. While I lifted weights, ran five days a week, and was open to trying pretty radical techniques when it came to exercise, I was quite stubborn when it came to altering the way I'd been eating for the previous 15 years.

I was reluctant—and hey, maybe even a little jealous—as she told me about the success of other people she knew who had adopted this new diet. (Of course it wasn't really "new"—the high-protein diet had been around for decades and was already favored by many bodybuilders and athletes.) But I finally broke down and agreed to try it for a few months to see what would happen. I began eating smaller meals every three hours, four times a day, consisting mainly of protein with some high-fiber carbohydrates in the form of oats, beans, fruits, and vegetables.

I was amazed—she was right. In a short period of time, my body fat decreased and lean muscle tissue increased, and I hadn't changed my exercise routine at all. (For more information on this type of diet, see Bill Phillips's book *Body For Life*. Barry Sears's book *The Zone* offers a modified approach to this eating plan as well.)

While there's no one plan that's ideal for everyone, this way of eating is the closest thing to perfection for me. Here's a simplified example of the typical meals I began to consume on a daily basis, which transformed my body into one that was leaner and more muscular:

Meal One (9:00 A.M.)
coffee
protein shake (I prefer Labrada or Myoplex brands), blended
   with water or organic skim milk
1 cup frozen fruit

Snack
1 piece whole-wheat toast
1 tablespoon peanut butter

Meal Two (noon)
12 ounces canned tuna (packed in water)
2 tablespoons light mayonnaise
romaine lettuce
1 tomato
2 slices whole-wheat bread

Meal Three (3 P.M.)
1 protein bar
½ to 1 cup mixed nuts
1 apple
(I sometimes add half a bagel here as well)

Meal Four (6 P.M.)
½ pound tuna, grilled
½ pound frozen broccoli, steamed
1 cup pasta
½ cup marinara sauce

(I also consume 1 to 2 gallons of water over the course of a
normal day.)

This was quite a radical change from my old high-carbohydrate diet—and the way my body changed in three months was radical, too.

In contrast, here is what my former high-carbohydrate diet looked like:

Snack (9:00 A.M.)
coffee or juice

Meal One (10:00 A.M.)
2 whole-wheat bagels or cereal with banana

Meal Two (noon)
tuna-salad sandwich
1 apple

Snack (3:00 P.M.)
2 whole-wheat bagels with mozzarella cheese

Meal Three (8:00 P.M.)
¼ pound pasta (that's a *huge* amount of pasta), topped with
    butter or marinara sauce and Parmesan cheese
1 pound frozen vegetables

As you can tell, this diet consisted mainly of carbohydrates. And regardless of how hard I trained, I rarely saw any noticeable changes in my physique.

Today, I try to consume one gram of protein for each pound of my body weight per day. This equals 185 grams of protein a day, broken up into each of the four meals I eat. So on average, my goal is to consume about 45 grams of protein at every meal. If I don't hit that number exactly, I try to make up for what I've missed with additional snacks. Fruits, vegetables, and carbohydrates such as oatmeal, whole-wheat or spinach pasta, and brown rice round out the foods I eat on a daily basis.

You can use my diet as a guideline to help you structure your day with multiple meals and possibly more protein at each one. (Be sure to add extra protein to your daily plan *gradually*, as some people may experience temporary bloating or excessive gas if they add too much protein too quickly.) I've never really been one to count calories, but if that works for you, continue to do so. Try a variety of foods and portion sizes until you find the program that works for you.

❋

Getting into the habit of eating a high-protein diet will take a little planning and a little patience, but it's worth it. The best way to begin is by charting your meals. Write down the time of your first meal each day, and then jot down in three-hour intervals when you should be eating next. Eat even if you're not hungry—when you let too much time go between meals, your blood sugar levels may drop dramatically, leading to hunger surges and overeating. So get and stay on a schedule of eating every three hours. Slow down and give it a shot.

REAL PEOPLE, REAL RESULTS

As we incorporate more lean protein, vegetables, and fruits into our diets, our bodies begin to lose fat, especially if coupled with a sound exercise program. The following are just a handful of the success stories I've heard over the years from people who have fine-tuned their diets to get the results they wanted.

One time, a woman called my radio show and said that she'd devoted the previous year to a strenuous five-day-a-week exercise program. While she'd had good results, she wanted to see more for all the hard work she was doing. She'd heard me discussing my eating plan, but her friends— including a nutrition expert—told her that eating this way only works for athletes, not "common folk." I explained to her that if her current diet was working for her, she should stick with it, but if it wasn't, what did she have to lose? Two months later, this same women called back to say that my plan worked so well for her that she was considering entering an amateur fitness competition in her hometown.

My brother, Terry, saw similar results within 30 days as well. He cut down on the simple carbohydrates that so may of us basically live on, such as low-fiber cereal, crackers, pasta, breads, cookies, and other sweets, and by doing so, managed to decrease his body fat more quickly than he ever believed was possible. Needless to say, my brother is now a huge proponent of this way of eating.

Dennis, a successful businessperson and a client of mine, wanted to drop some body fat and get back into shape. Accustomed to long workdays, he adopted a high-protein, frequent-meal diet and was amazed at how, within the first month, his energy level increased so dramatically.

Another client, Mark, also received many benefits from eating this way, as well as embarking on a strong fitness program. He lost a significant amount of weight and gained more energy. In addition, his cravings for sweets (he loved M&M's) decreased as well.

The same can happen to you. Slow down—change the way you think about eating, then change the way you eat to transform your body.

THE EFFECT OF WATER ON YOUR HEALTH

The next important change you need to make to boost your energy level and improve your overall health is to consume much more water than most people do on a daily basis. The *Journal of the American Dietetic Association* published a study that explained a formula used for determining the amount of water you need to drink each day, and it far exceeds the often-recommended eight glasses per day. To find out how much you really need, multiply your weight (in pounds) by .04, and then double that result. This amount is the number of eight-ounce glasses of water needed per day for a sedentary person. That means that if you weigh 185 pounds, you'd need to drink about 15 glasses of water a day. If you exercise regularly, I'd add another eight to ten glasses. It seems like a lot because it is!

One of the best books to read on this subject is *Our Body's Many Cries For Water*, by Fereydoon Batmanghelidj, M.D. Every time I interviewed Dr. Batmanghelidj on my radio show, I'd get a ton of phone calls and e-mails from listeners who wanted to share the amazing results they experienced once they began drinking more water.

I remember one e-mail from a listener who had suffered from serious heartburn for years. After going through a battery of tests and medications, all to no avail, his doctor recommended surgery. While there was no guarantee that this would remedy his problem, he'd run out of options. His condition had become so severe that it interfered with his life not only during his waking hours, but while he tried to sleep as well.

After listening to an interview with Dr. Batmanghelidj, this gentleman decided to see if his condition might be caused by a lack of water intake. After drinking an increased amount of water for two weeks, his problem disappeared. Much to the amazement of his doctors, this man was medication free after 30 days—his condition had been due to what Dr. Batmanghelidj calls "a simple form of dehydration." Can you imagine the joy this man felt after suffering for so long with this condition? His energy level shot up immediately, and as you can imagine, so did his level of health and happiness.

Increasing your daily water intake doesn't have to happen all at once. My sister, Marydianne, who is an elementary school teacher, began simply by keeping a large glass of flavored seltzer water on her desk and sipping it throughout the day. Now her goal is to finish at least two of these extra-large glasses by the end of each afternoon.

Due to the fact that water plays such a huge role in maintaining optimal health, I'd like you to begin charting the amount that you drink on a daily basis. Using the formula suggested by the American Dietetic Association (.04 x your body weight x 2), estimate the number of eight-ounce glasses that you should be consuming per day. Then keep track of your water consumption for the next week.

❋

One day, as I was ordering a sandwich from a Subway shop in Gainesville, Florida, I got a wonderful surprise. The man behind the counter who had been taking my order looked up and asked me if I'd ever done radio voice-overs, as I sounded very familiar to him. When I told him no, but that for nine years I hosted a national radio show, he started laughing. "David Essel," he said, "you helped me stay on the football team at a small college in Georgia."

The man went on to tell me how he used to listen to my show while he delivered pizzas on weekends. He'd always struggled to maintain the weight his coaches required— that is, until he began listening to the advice I gave about drinking water and eating frequent meals. Although he wasn't a fan of plain water, he found that he could drink plenty of *flavored* water, which helped keep his appetite in check. He also started eating smaller meals throughout the day and snacking on flavored rice cakes, which also satisfied his appetite. He told me that these two tips helped him stay at his desired weight and keep his position on the team. It was a great conversation, and proof again that we all need to slow down and adopt new strategies in life when the ones we have aren't working.

THE WONDER OF NUTRITIONAL SUPPLEMENTS

Because there are many exceptional books on nutrition available today, I won't offer a list of supplements that may positively affect all the health conditions you may have. Instead, I'd like to share my personal daily supplement regime with you, as well as stories from clients and former radio listeners who have achieved great success through the addition of nutritional supplements to their health routine.

These products should be seen for what they are— *supplements* to an excellent diet. I don't recommend taking any pill in place of developing healthy eating habits, for it's best to get the vitamins and minerals that you need from the food you eat. Choose organically certified products whenever possible, drink plenty of water every day, and then, on top of all of the other health habits that we've discussed in this book, take the best nutritional supplements you can find.

(What I'm discussing in this chapter should not take the place of your doctor's advice. Some herbs can have a harmful effect when taken with prescription drugs or when there's a preexisting medical condition. Always ask your doctor or pharmacist about possible interactions before you take any supplements.)

I can't tell you how many success stories I heard from listeners over the nine years I was on the air with respect to the power of nutritional supplementation—they would undoubtedly run into the thousands. People who had battled chronic conditions for decades with no relief were getting incredible results after just three to six months of nutritional supplementation. (Remember: It's essential to check with your physician prior to taking any vitamins or herbal supplements.)

One woman called to tell me about the positive effect that the herb feverfew had on her headaches. She'd suffered from debilitating migraines for more than 15 years, and the medication she'd been prescribed didn't seem to help. Within a month of taking standardized feverfew capsules a few times a day, her migraines were reduced in severity and frequency.

Another time, I got a call from a man who had struggled with prostate problems for years (common symptoms of prostate problems include frequent urination at night and not feeling that the bladder is empty after urinating). Hoping for some form of relief, he opted for surgery. But after hearing about the benefits of saw palmetto on my show, he talked to his doctor about delaying his surgery and giving the herb a chance to improve his condition. Well, 60 days later, his symptoms had decreased so dramatically that the procedure was canceled.

Many people suffer from tinnitus, a constant ringing in the ears. But I had no idea how many folks are affected by this condition until I started sharing studies about the effects of ginkgo biloba on my show. One woman, who had been challenged by this sensation for over 30 years, called to tell me that there was a noticeable change in her condition after taking ginkgo biloba for just one month. She was ecstatic to have found something that offered relief.

The last example I'd like to share came from another caller who hadn't been able to relieve his chronic nasal congestion. After hearing about the potential benefits of the herb stinging nettle on my show, he decided to give it a try. Within 90 days, he called to report a 75 percent reduction in his congestive symptoms.

I think you get the picture. I've seen too many positive changes in people's lives to believe that these products don't work. Results may vary, but if you want to give yourself the best shot at living the healthiest life possible, I believe nutritional supplementation should be a priority.

With your doctor, explore the myriad nutritional supplements that just might improve your health. For additional information on herbs, please refer to the following books:

- *Prescription for Nutritional Healing: A Practical A–Z Reference to Drug-Free Remedies Using Vitamins, Minerals, Herbs, and Food Supplements*, by Phyllis A. Balch and James F. Balch, M.D. (Avery, 2000).

- *Encyclopedia of Nutritional Supplements: The Essential Guide for Improving Your Health Naturally*, by Michael T. Murray (Prima Publishing, 1996).

Since in some cases it may take 60 to 90 days for herbs to take effect, slow down as nature does all it can to help your body heal and balance itself. The "slow down" message is coming at us from all angles, isn't it? In our fast-paced world of "Take it now and feel better in 20 minutes," even Mother Nature knows that good things sometimes take time.

MY DAILY NUTRITIONAL PROGRAM

Even though my life, like almost everyone else's, is very hectic and stressful at times, I rarely get sick. I believe a primary reason for that is the amount and variety of nutritional supplements I've been taking for the past 20 years.

It's my opinion that supplements work best if the recommended dosages are split and taken twice per day (unless otherwise indicated). This allows your body the opportunity to have these nutrients available at all times.

The following is a list of the supplements I currently take, along with a very brief description of the benefits I hope to gain from them:

MORNING SUPPLEMENTS (upon waking up, 20 minutes before breakfast)	
Supplement	Benefit
2,000 mg. vitamin C	Immune-system health
175 mg. milk thistle extract (Nature's Way Thisilyn brand)	Liver health

DAILY SUPPLEMENTS (taken after meals)	
Supplement	Benefit
Multivitamin/mineral (Alive! brand) (2 capsules in the A.M., 1 in the P.M.)	Overall health enhancement
Fish oil (Fisol brand) (2 capsules in the A.M.)	Omega-3 fatty acids for heart, joint, and skin health
Cacao (whole-bean supplement) (2 capsules in the A.M.)	Mild stimulant, beneficial antioxidants, and flavanoids similar to the ones found in green tea
Saw palmetto (1 capsule in the A.M., 1 in the P.M.)	Prostate health, urinary flow (for men)
Immunity capsules (StayWell brand)	Immune-system functioning
Hawthorne extract (Nature's Way Heartcare brand) (1 capsule in the A.M., 1 in the P.M.)	Heart health
Maca extract (2 capsules in the A.M., 1 in the P.M.)	Energy, physical stamina
Calcium and magnesium (750 mg. calcium, 300 mg. magnesium, half in the A.M. and half in the P.M.)	Bone, tooth, muscle, and heart health

DAILY SUPPLEMENTS (taken after meals) cont.	
Supplement	Benefit
Flax oil (organic) (2 capsules in the A.M., 1 in the P.M.)	Heart, immune-system, and hormonal-system health
Phosphatidylserine (2 capsules in the A.M., 1 in the P.M.)	Brain functioning (may delay brain deterioration caused by aging)
Neuromins DHA (2 capsules in the A.M., 1 in the P.M.)	Brain and visual functioning
Bilberry extract (Nature's Way brand) (2 capsules in the A.M., 1 in the P.M.)	Eye health

BEFORE BEDTIME	
Supplement	Benefit
2,000 mg. psyllium fiber	Colon health

This nutritional supplementation program has had a major impact on my overall health, and I believe that supplements can do the same for you. Slow down and look at what you desire for your mind and body and begin to make the changes necessary today to bring your goals to fruition. Everything is possible, but only if you slow down and do it.

✳ ✳ ✳

Part III Review

Exercise, diet, and nutritional supplementation are the power-packed trio that if used regularly will help you get the body, energy, and health you've always wanted. By changing your exercise and nutritional practices, you really can achieve the health goals that may have seemed unattainable at one time.

Take a moment or two to slow down and review the information presented in Part III. Remember that the writing exercises are truly the hidden gems of this work, and your written answers at the end of each part of this book will help you focus, create the intention to change, and then propel you forward as you set your action plan into motion.

The act of writing allows you to delve deeper into your mind to recall from the previous pages the information that was important to *you* and relevant to *your* life and desires. I believe that this is one of the many powerful steps that you can take in order to create the life you desire. So slow down, think, write, and then become who you truly want to be.

Please answer the following questions:

1. What was covered, in detail, in this section?

———————————————————————————————

———————————————————————————————

———————————————————————————————

———————————————————————————————

2. What was of most interest to you, and why?

_____

_____

_____

_____

3. What's the current plan of action you'll institute to help you achieve your goal? (Specifically list the steps you'll take to live the life you really want to.)

_____

_____

_____

_____

After finishing these questions, move ahead to Part IV, where you'll slow down to enhance your spiritual connection.

❊ ❊ ❊

PART IV

Slow Down
to Enhance Your
Spiritual Connection

chapter 8

Living a Centered Life

One of life's greatest achievements is finding the path that leads to a more centered, spiritual existence, in which you feel connected to your God, or your true essence. You'll know when you've found your path because a sense of peace will overcome your being—many people describe this feeling as connectedness, bliss, nirvana, or an encounter with their creator. But don't be fooled into thinking that this experience has to continue 24 hours a day for it to be meaningful. In fact, if you expect to constantly operate in the "I'm one with God and the universe" state, you'll probably end up living in frustration.

I'd like to propose a different goal—one that may even be attainable by this afternoon, next week, or next month at the latest—that will connect you to your center, core, or spirit. Now, initially the connection may be fleeting, but over time it can grow stronger and stronger until it becomes a regular part of your day-to-day existence. The goal is to live the most centered life possible, and to release any attachment to the expectation that this experience will last 365 days a year. If it does, rejoice—but if it doesn't (and for many of us, it may not), you can still relish the moments it does happen and spend the rest of your time at peace with who you are.

The end result of pursuing this centered life is living in harmony with yourself—with your victories as well as your setbacks. You'll still have ups and downs, but your negative response to challenging experiences will be lessened; and you'll react to the outside world with more compassion, empathy, and grace.

When you slow down and move to your source through prayer, meditation, and other rituals, you become aware of the possibility of living a more centered life. Of course you'll still feel pushed in the opposite direction at times, as pressure at work or at home can consume your thoughts and lead you away from your spirit. So make a habit of asking yourself, "Am I connected to my source today? And if not, what can I do about that right now?"

While I'm still a major work in progress, the benefits I've seen when I focus on this centered approach have been phenomenal. Challenges such as losing money in investments, encountering disagreements in relationships, or dealing with obstacles in my career would have thrown me into emotional chaos before, but now I can see them for what they are: minor bumps in the road of life.

CENTER YOURSELF, CHANGE YOUR WORLD

One of the ways you can judge if your life is being lived with a connection to your source is how others respond to you. For example, I remember a time when a close friend and I hit a wall in our relationship, and we struggled over an issue right before she had to leave for a trip. The next day, I found myself off center—away from my spirit. Yet the minute I realized what I'd done to myself by allowing our difference of opinion to consume my thoughts, things started to shift. This awareness was the first step needed to help me reconnect with my center. I started mentally sending her love, and as I sat in a church courtyard praying, I wrote her a short letter explaining my sorrow over our disagreement. When she returned from her trip, I gave her the letter, and while she was too far into her frustration to understand my intention, I began to feel more balanced.

Later that same day, after filming some segments for a television show I was hosting, the producer started sharing some professional difficulties he was facing at the moment. He opened up quickly, and was very appreciative of my willingness to listen. Two days later, another friend who had rarely shared any of her desires or dreams in life began telling me some of her long-buried hopes and wishes. Then, while in a market that I frequent, a cashier who had never smiled or communicated with me before gave me a big hello as I entered the store. I knew then that even if I hadn't totally resolved the personal issues at hand, I'd begun to move back to my source.

When your energy and spirit are revolving at a higher and healthier level, they're reflected back to you by the people you come in contact with. What became evident from my experience was that when I slowed down and placed myself in the spiritual surroundings of a church courtyard during a time of personal frustration, I immediately brought myself back to my center. Instead of holding on to the thought, *I'm right, and you're wrong,* I went deeper and tried to release my own negative emotions. Once I was able to do so, my world was instantly altered, and the reactions of the people around me proved that I had returned to a balanced state.

It's Never Too Late

When you feel lost, you have the tendency to doubt yourself and live life with little faith. But no matter how long you've felt disconnected, you can return to your source. My client Sheryl felt deeply separated from her spiritual side due to a tragic accident that took the life of her younger sister. Her story can open your eyes to the wonders of recovery and love.

When I began working with David, I hated God, and I hadn't been to church in nearly three decades. Twenty-eight years ago, when I was a senior in high school, I witnessed my 12-year-old sister being slammed into head-on by a drunk driver while she was helping a younger child cross the highway. She landed on some crushed rock, her neck was broken, and she died instantly. The driver didn't even stop.

Everyone told me that it was "God's will." I refused to accept that. How could God take the life of this beautiful, loving, vibrant, red-haired little girl who was just beginning to live life? So I completely blocked God out.

Through my writing and my coaching sessions with David, I realized that it wasn't God that I hated so much—it was myself. I felt guilty for not being able to save my sister's life, and I'd suppressed that feeling for a very long time. I knew that I needed to let God back into my life—I'd left Him, but He had always been with me.

I've opened my heart wide to God again, and some of the most beautiful things have happened and continue to happen every day. I've seen and heard God talk to me in so many different ways—something I thought could only happen to ministers, priests, and other spiritual leaders. I've heard God speak to me through the sunshine on a cold and cloudy day, the beautiful sunrise and sunsets with all their amazing colors, and creative talents I've discovered that I never thought I had. But God talks to me the loudest and the clearest when I'm sitting on the beach, watching and listening to the ocean waves with all of their calm and peacefulness. When I'm near the ocean, God speaks to me through poetry, and although I've never thought of myself as a poet, the words come to me so quickly that it's really hard to write them down fast enough.

During one coaching session with David, I could feel this bubble of total peace encircle me. I felt as if I were being lifted up and having an out-of-body experience—floating above and feeling no pain or stress. I was looking down on myself talking on the phone, and I had no idea what was happening to me. When I described to David what I was feeling, he told me it was called <u>transcendence.</u> It was the most glorious and heavenly feeling of peacefulness—I never wanted it to end. I felt God's presence all around me.

By opening myself up and letting the sunshine fill me with warmth again, I know now that God loves me unconditionally. He is always with me; I just need to remember to let Him in.

THE POWER OF PRAYER

What is prayer? Some say it's a way to petition God's grace or forgiveness, or to "ask earnestly" for something. But daily prayer can also be used to show gratitude, effect healing, or express remorse. It's the simple act of communicating with an ever-present, ever-loving life force, which has been called God, Buddha, Allah, and a higher power. Prayer is often defined as a purely religious ritual or form of communication, but some individuals also focus their prayers within, asking themselves to be guided to a greater awareness so that every act and thought is the "right" one.

I believe that some people have misinterpreted prayer or inner communication as something to be done in a church or temple only, and because of this, they don't use it as regularly as they could. Others may think that it just isn't "cool" to pray, or if they were forced to pray as children, they may still be rebelling against their parents by refusing to do so today. Perhaps even more common is the belief that if one's prayers aren't answered as expected, then time spent in prayer was wasted.

Yet there are many benefits to these daily inner conversations, and our lives can be helped from *more* time in prayer, not less. Praying allows us to take a break from the fast-paced life so many of us lead. It's a conscious act that we take part in to build a stronger foundation with who we are and what we want to become. When we pray, we become more grounded and centered, which allows us to tap in to a powerful energy force within—and enables us to have a more positive impact on the outside world. Our spirit is enhanced, optimism can grow, and a sense of "lightness" fills our existence.

Just as a love relationship needs the strongest of foundations to be able to handle the stress and challenges that come with being a couple, we all need the power and connectedness that prayer offers in order to lead a more centered and spiritual life. Through the deepening that occurs with daily prayer, we find ourselves more able to work through the challenges and discomforts life presents, and at the same time, rejoice in the good things that come our way.

IS THERE A CORRECT WAY TO PRAY?

When I was growing up, I was encouraged to pray at the traditional times and places: before bed, before dinner, and at church on Sunday. When my life began to change a number of years ago through my desire to connect more deeply with myself and discover why I'm here and how I can help others, prayer became a daily ritual. I wanted to be in union with my spirit and my God more often, so prayer became a constant companion.

One of the questions people regularly asked on my radio show was, "Is there a correct way to pray?" At times I would think, *Gosh, after all of these years of praying, I sure hope I haven't been doing it wrong!* So whenever I interviewed religious and spiritual experts, such as priests, rabbis, or Buddhist monks, I loved to pose this question to them to see what answers they might offer to enlighten not just my listeners, but myself as well.

There was a part of me back then that thought that each of these individuals, being from such varied religious backgrounds, must have very different beliefs about prayer. I was surprised to learn that they all believed the following to be true: *When you pray, ask for all that you desire—a better job, the perfect mate, great wealth, improved health, and so on. Then, at the end of your prayer, release your need for the end result to come to fruition, and be thankful for all that you have.* Period. That was it.

I was shocked and relieved all at once. After taking some time to digest their definition, it began to make sense. We often erroneously believe that our life would be just phenomenal if we could only attract a specific outcome. We pray for this to be manifested so that we'll finally be happy, successful, and living a joyful life. But when we hold on so dearly to the end result and it doesn't happen the way we expect it to, we end up with frustration and unhappiness.

Let me put it this way: Have you ever prayed for a large sum of money, hoping that the security of having a lot of cash would end all your struggles? Well, if you've done this, it might surprise you to know that a survey conducted a number of years ago showed that close to 40 percent of lottery winners are broke and back to work within five years of their big payday. Stories of poor health, stress, broken families, and shattered dreams abound for individuals who believed that money was the answer to their problems. The reason for this is simple: If we're constantly living our life in the future, desperately wanting the love, money, or success that has eluded us up to now, how can we be centered and connected to our spirit in the present? It's just not possible. Yet so may times we leave a centered way of living and wish for a different existence. By doing so, we risk missing out on the many beautiful daily experiences that pop up all around us.

MANY ANSWERS TO PRAYERS

If you stop for a moment and realize that one of the benefits of a life based in prayer is that you may live more peacefully, isn't this enough? If you can drive down the road, engaged in a beautiful and conscious inner dialogue, and simply thank the sun and the trees for their existence, isn't this a wonderful reason to live a life in prayer? If you use prayer to ask for assistance, which I believe you should do daily, and combine your requests with thoughts of gratitude, you can lighten your spirits regardless of what challenges you're currently facing, and this alone will help you become more centered.

My client Jody faced many personal and career challenges over the last several years and didn't know how to tap in to the amazing internal strength that she already had—that is, until she started using prayer on a daily basis. Here's her story:

> *I suppose I always thought of a state of grace as something more phenomenal than what I've experienced—such as when a yogi reaches nirvana. Yet when I reflect on my life over the past few years, I see such an incredible transformation that I suppose where I am now could be considered a state of grace. I'm reminded of the story of Exodus, when Moses came to the Hebrews, who were slaves in Egypt, and told them that God wanted to free them from their bondage. They had been slaves there for many years, and had the "slave mentality" that one acquires from being beaten down and oppressed. Yet once they allowed themselves to believe in God and His power to transform the world, that's exactly what happened. And so it has been in my life.*
>
> *Once I was able to connect with God through prayer, everything in my life shifted. I feel so much like when the Red Sea parted and the Hebrews walked through it, with the Egyptian army pursuing them. Just as they reached dry land, the sea came together again and the army was wiped out! I feel as though I've come through the Red Sea myself, and can really taste the sweetness of freedom.*
>
> *Free is what I feel—free of the oppression that was hanging over my head like a black cloud for the last ten years when I was with my ex-husband. I don't think I ever realized how heavy that cloud was until it lifted. Like the Hebrew slaves, I knew that I was suffering, but I was so*

accustomed to that feeling that I didn't know that it could be any different. It's not just that I've been released from the relationship, it's also that I've been set free of my own fear.

So what does the state of grace feel like? It's an inner contentment, a sense that things are as they should be. It's a feeling of joy from all the simple things in life, and an appreciation of everything I have—my life, my son, and my family. There's no longer the feeling that <u>Oh, if only I could fix this, then everything would be all right.</u> It's not because everything is perfect—it isn't. It's because I'm feeling a huge appreciation of what I <u>do</u> have, and knowing that what needs to come, will. It's about trust in myself and God.

So how do I hold on to that state of grace and not lose sight of it? It's about staying in a place of gratitude. I've kept a gratitude journal, and every night or morning, I write down five things I'm thankful for on that day. This is one tool I can use to keep my awareness at a heightened level, and not to take things for granted.

✳

I've heard it said many times that prayers are answered in one of three ways: yes, no, or maybe. If this is true, then every prayer you pray is immediately answered in one way or another!

WHERE TO DIALOGUE, WHERE TO PRAY

Another question I've been frequently asked is: "Isn't prayer taken more seriously if it's offered in a religious or spiritual building, or on holy ground?" My instinct says that you should pray where you are, regardless of where that may be. While I have no evidence to prove that this is true, it just seems logical that if your inner connection is to God (or your higher power), which is everywhere and in everything, how could He (or She) not hear your prayers, regardless of where you are physically? If this same dialogue is to your own inner being, does it matter where you pray? If people feel that they need to be in some sort of religious edifice to pray, yet their schedules don't allow them this freedom during the certain hours that the doors are open, couldn't they still benefit from daily dialogue, regardless of where they are?

I try to pray to God and my own inner core throughout each day. As I drive in my car, I'll turn off the radio for periods of time and stay within the reflection of prayer. When I wake up, I'll often lie in bed and ask to be stronger and more loving. I also love the connection I receive from within and above as I sit in an empty church or the courtyard of a temple (some of the most peaceful moments I've ever experienced have been when I was alone in one of these two locations).

Plan a day this week—tomorrow might be perfect—to begin a deeper connection or dialogue with yourself. At lunch tomorrow, find a quiet, private space and pray for just five minutes. Slow down to connect with your true spirit.

Praying for Others

Over the past several years, I've gotten into the habit of saying prayers for others as well as myself. In my radio days, I used to say a prayer for my one million listeners prior to the beginning of each of my shows. I'd pray that my energy and words would help them in all ways possible, and I'd ask to maximize my potential during the program. When I'm filming on a television set, I do the same thing. Before I work with someone in person or on the phone, I say a prayer and bless myself with the sign of the cross, asking to benefit that client's growth, health, and safety. Then I ask that this person be able to see the inner reflection and beauty of who he or she truly is. Even before business meetings and calls, I repeat the same ritual. I know that this act of inner dialogue or prayer calms me, centers me, slows me down, and helps me focus on the task at hand. It helps turn every event in life into an opportunity to reconnect with my spirit.

Many people have written eloquently on the power of sending positive energy to everyone you meet in the hopes of raising their awareness and joy in life. In his book *There's a Spiritual Solution to Every Problem*, Wayne Dyer discusses the concept of bringing our vibrational energy core to new heights so that we may live the life of a more enlightened person. He talks about the power of sending loving thoughts to everyone we meet—even the homeless person lying by the side of the road. We can all use our inner voice to send loving thoughts. After all, isn't that one of the greatest forms of prayer available?

If you're still skeptical about the power of prayer or the effectiveness of using inner dialogue to help create a positive change in the outside world, I ask you to read *Prayer Is Good Medicine*, by Larry Dossey, M.D. After reading this book and then interviewing Dr. Dossey several times, I'm more convinced than ever that we need to find ways to fill our day with prayers to help heal the world, ourselves, and our loved ones.

The fact is that throughout the ages, prayer has been used as a form of medicine to help people heal. But until recently, many folks in the medical establishment refused to believe that prayer could be studied and proven effective in the same way that penicillin could. But studies have now been formulated to take a closer look at the power of prayer, and the outcome may astound you. In San Francisco, a stringent, double-blind study was done using prayer to see if it would help in the recovery rate of patients after heart surgery. None of the patients knew that they were being prayed for, and the results were unbelievable. The "prayed for" group had fewer postsurgical complications and needed less medication than the control group. Another study, led by Dr. Elisabeth Targ, looked at the effect of distant prayer on AIDS patients. In the control group of patients *not* receiving prayer over a specific period of time, 40 percent died. However, during the same time period, no one in the prayed-for group died. (These two examples can both be found in Dr. Dossey's book.)

As if these studies weren't enough to prove that a deep connection to our source or core can enhance our ability to heal, check out this headline from an article in *USA Today* (March 19, 2002): "AIDS Cocktail: Medicine, Faith and Trust." The article stated that "long-term AIDS survivors are far more likely than those whose disease progresses faster to be caring altruists with strong spiritual faith and trust in their doctors . . ."

It seems to me that if connecting to their spiritual side can help cardiac and AIDS patients, then the same approach will work for you and me, regardless of what we might be challenged by in life.

According to Dr. Dossey, there's no one way to pray that's more effective than another. The key is intention. If you focus on asking your higher power for guidance, love, and the outcome that's appropriate for you at this time, your intention is pure, and the best opportunity will come.

❉

Many people find an untapped resource of love and compassion after going through some very rough stages in life. Stay open to the potential healing properties of prayer, and use this wonderful technique daily. However, balance is key: Don't forego medical treatment for an illness or addiction if that's what's needed. Simply add prayer as one more tool in helping yourself or others along the path of life.

Slow down, connect to your center, and transform your life today.

❉ ❉ ❉

chapter 9

Maximizing Your Life with Meditation and Rituals

A long with the act of prayer or inner dialogue, the easiest and most direct way to slow down is through the use of meditation. Every client I've worked with over the years has benefited greatly from using this technique in their search for a more connected, peaceful life. Many were truly astonished by the end result they experienced, and their lives became more focused and centered. Why they came to work with me didn't matter, as they all discovered that many of the answers they were looking for could only be found by going within themselves through the use of this daily practice.

My first experience with meditation was in 1974, when I was invited to a Transcendental Meditation (TM) introductory class while a student at Syracuse University. I was a stereotypical jock back then, and I wanted nothing to do with some weird mystical practice that people claimed could enhance your health, keep you young, reduce stress, and increase your creativity. I probably stayed in the room for about 45 seconds. Watching all the people we called "granola heads" sitting in a circle "doing nothing" seemed like a waste of time. I felt like a fish out of water, but I later found out that *I* was the one who wasted years before I began to experience the benefits of daily meditation. And all those claims they made about the benefits of meditation? Well, they turned out to be scientifically valid.

As a matter of fact, the art of meditation has even been studied by our own government. The National Institutes of Health studied the effect of meditation versus prescription drugs on high blood pressure a number of years ago. Without making any changes to diet or exercise, both therapies lowered blood pressure equally—there was no significant difference between the group that practiced TM twice a day for 20 minutes and the group that took blood-pressure-lowering medication. Now, the great news for the meditation group was that they experienced no negative side effects caused by medication, and there was no ongoing monthly cost for prescription refills.

Studies on the power of TM to reduce cigarette, drug, and alcohol use have also revealed some incredible results. Reviews in *Alcoholism Treatment Quarterly* (11: 13–87, 1994) and *International Journal of the Addictions* (26: 293–325, 1991) showed that those utilizing TM in their attempts to abstain from these substances experienced a success rate of between 51 and 89 percent over 18- and 22-month periods. According to these studies, many conventional abstinence programs' success rates begin to decrease sharply by three months after the programs have been implemented.

With respect to the effect that daily meditation has on reversing the aging process, a study reported in the *International Journal of Neuroscience* in 1982 showed that individuals who had been practicing TM for five years or more were physiologically 12 years younger than their chronological age! These are just a few of the studies that prove how beneficial meditation can be to our health. But what about its effect on our search for centeredness? Daily meditation, which I've been doing since 1988 in one form or another, has changed my life. It's given me a calmer perspective and more insight than I could have ever imagined. It's hard to believe that because of the stigma that surrounds the word *meditation*, I initially shied away from doing it, and would even tell others that I thought it was a waste of time. I didn't understand how anyone could benefit from a technique that has them sitting around doing "nothing." Little did I know how wrong I could be.

I began my exploration of the power of meditation by listening to audiocassettes on the subject. Over the years, I've tried hundreds of different meditation techniques, and I don't believe that there's only one true way to meditate—I think they're all valid. If you find a way that works for you, stick with it. Please don't buy into someone else's belief that their form is necessarily the right one for you, too—experience it for yourself. Investigate the world of meditative options, and then go for the one you connect with most.

GETTING STARTED

For me, meditation is a period of cleansing, releasing, and being with myself without expectation. It slows me down in several ways:

- I step out of "normal" hectic living and create a sacred space and time.

- As I sit or lie down, my body relaxes.

- I go within myself and connect with my spirit.

I have yet to find any other activity that actually allows me to do all of this in such a short period of time.

Speaking of time, I once got a call on my radio show from a woman who felt stymied in her approach to meditation because she couldn't do it for 30 minutes straight. She asked, "To be a good meditator, how long should I be able to do it, how often, what position should I be in, and where?" In Chapter 8, I said that prayer or inner dialogue is a way to communicate with God, a higher power, or your true self. Meditation, on the other hand, has been referred to as the opening that allows that communication to occur. So I believe that once again, we need to find our *own* way, regardless of what the experts might say.

First of all, anyone who attempts to meditate is already a "good meditator." I hate to think of how many people might have stopped meditating because they feared they weren't doing it right. Please, drop the self-judgment and relax! Many studies have been done on groups of people who meditate twice a day for 20 minutes at a time, so set this as a goal if you'd like, but remember that *any* time spent in meditation equals a successful session. If you begin with an egg timer and breathe deeply for just one minute, that's a start. Add a minute a week until you reach 20 to 25 minutes and see how you feel afterward. My guess is that you'll be so much more connected and centered that you'll continue practicing the technique forever.

When you're first starting out, you can listen to a meditation audio program if it helps. (I've produced a tape called *No More Stress: A Relaxation and Meditation Program for Your Health and Happiness*. For more information, please go to my Website: **www.davidessel.com**.) Since most people aren't used to sitting in silence, those who begin this way are often successful because someone else's voice leads them through each session. Also, check out techniques such as Transcendental Meditation (**www.tm.com**) to see if this is one that you enjoy doing. Slow down, breathe deeply, and *feel* into the form of meditation that's right for you.

You may choose to use a mantra, which is a word or sound that you mentally or verbally repeat during your meditation session. It might be one that you chose (such as "love," "one," "sun," or "om") or one that's given to you by a mentor, guru, or meditation organization. Many have defined the mantra as the vehicle that takes you from your day-to-day existence in the outside world to the peacefulness and bliss that resides within your center. Like the bus or taxi that takes you from one side of the city to another, the mantra is the vehicle leading you to the core of who you are.

The slowing down that naturally occurs through the regular use of meditation will give you a sense of connectedness to the beauty of your inner world. But don't be discouraged if other thoughts arise during each session, too, such as, "I'm hungry," "I have to pick up the kids in an hour," or "The bills are due, but we don't have enough money." Don't see these thoughts as something to avoid. Instead, just accept them as they are. Your session isn't a failure just because worldly concerns have invaded your silent space. Simply observe these thoughts and then let them go, returning to your breathing or the repetition of your mantra.

So, is there a correct time and place to meditate? I say that the best time is whenever you have a moment, and the best place is wherever you are. When I worked as a spokesperson for a resort in Puerto Vallarta, Mexico, I met a massage therapist who was into meditation. He told me that he used to think it should always be done in a private, quiet setting. Yet during his training with several masters, he often saw them go into deep meditative states in public—

even on crowded buses. They taught him to let go of judging a place or time as being appropriate, and just meditate whenever and wherever. Eventually, this man became so adept that he even meditated on the corner of some of the busiest streets in Mexico City, one of the most populated cities in the world, for hours on end! Since meeting him, I've learned to utilize my time on airplanes to experience the wonderful benefits of meditation.

Think of all the locations where you can take advantage of downtime and meditate on a daily basis. Make a list of these places, regardless of how crazy they may seem to you at first. Here are a few to get you started:

- A dentist's or doctor's office

- Taxis, planes, buses, or subway trains

- Hair salons

Stay open to the benefits that meditation offers you, regardless of the time you have or where you are.

BREATH MEDITATION

One of the simplest ways to enter the world of meditation is by mentally following your breath in and out of your body. This should only take a few minutes to do. Sit comfortably, close your eyes, and beginning with your head, ask your body to relax all the way down to your toes. Mentally say, "My eyes are relaxed." Then breathe in and out. "My jaw is relaxed." Then breathe in and out. "My neck is relaxed." Breathe in and out until you've relaxed your entire body. Then, as you inhale, silently repeat the word *inhale*, and as you exhale, silently repeat the word *exhale*. Do this several times each day for just a few minutes at a time. Again, release the need to judge a session as good or bad. As thoughts arise, observe them and then let them go. As your mind relaxes, your body will follow, leading you to the way of your spirit.

Yes, sitting and doing nothing *can* yield great results, but only if you slow yourself down regularly to access your inner core. The connection with mind, body, and spirit that we're all searching for can be accessed in part through the art of meditation.

Lee, one of my clients, learned firsthand about the power of meditation. Here's his story:

> *I'd always been a type A personality, and I'd already watched my father and every male member of both sides of my family succumb to heart disease, but I became determined that this wouldn't happen to me. Yet even though I was very dedicated to proper exercise and nutrition, I knew something was missing—I felt as if some key component of a healthy lifestyle was eluding me. In working with David, I was more able to see the value of going within—that is, I was able to understand the value of what's commonly referred to as meditation.*
>
> *I'd dabbled with meditation before, but my driven personality always got in the way. The voice inside my head kept saying, "Don't just sit there, do something!" David helped me understand the value of slowing down. I can remember laughing with him one day as we talked about changing my inner voices's message to, "Don't just do something, sit there!"*

In casual conversation, we would compare notes on how our workouts were going and how our love lives were progressing. But it was always most interesting when our attention would turn to the amazing insights gained through our meditation sessions. Ironically, our moments of "non-doing" became some of our most productive times, and together we began to understand that by slowing down, we could actually accomplish more.

Through meditation, I was more able to observe my thought process. I watched my thoughts travel all over the map. But instead of evaluating or judging those thoughts as good, bad, silly, or brilliant, I learned to just note them and think, <u>Hmm, isn't that interesting.</u> Lo and behold, after several months of dedicated 15-minute meditation sessions, five to seven times per week, a dramatic change occurred. I could actually stop and examine my thoughts in real time. Before reacting with a cross remark to a loved one, I'd catch myself and think, <u>I wonder if I could respond differently here.</u> I found myself stopping before leaving the house and asking, "Do I have my keys and my wallet?" Now this may not seem like a big deal, but the cumulative effect was that my life became less of a struggle and infinitely more enjoyable.

Now, rather than having knee-jerk reactions to situations, I have the option to respond with some degree of awareness, and new options and possibilities for behavior have opened up. Are all my problems solved? Of course not. Is meditation a panacea for all life's ills? No. But if I were to pick one thing that has had the greatest impact on my life over the last ten years, it would definitely be meditation, and the slowing down that came with it.

SLOWING DOWN THROUGH THE USE OF RITUALS

Rituals have been used from the beginning of time to signify that it's time to slow down and shift one's attention to a specific event. The rituals of bar and bat mitzvah in the Jewish religion celebrate a young person's attainment of his or her 13th birthday, a time to reflect on the past and future. Christmas and the numerous rituals surrounding this day and the ones preceding it celebrate the birth of Christ. The wedding ceremony is full of rituals that lead the way for two people to unite in marriage, leaving behind the old, while looking forward to a new existence together. Rituals help us center ourselves and keep us headed on a strong spiritual path.

Amy was a client of mine from the West Coast who had read all the best-known self-help books and attended countless lectures, yet she still couldn't find the sense of connection she desired. After several sessions, I asked her what she thought someone who was centered would do regularly that she wasn't doing. Without even thinking, she blurted out, "They'd have some way to remind themselves daily to act or think in a way that reflected who they wanted to become." Her answer hit the nail on the head.

Most successful people create daily rituals to help themselves stay focused. It's been said that Ernest Hemingway sharpened 25 pencils every day before he began writing—a ritual designed to get him into the mind-set of his work. I've even heard of athletes who put their uniforms on in a certain sequence before games to help access their core. So I asked Amy to create a ritual to be performed before she got out of bed and again before she left work at the end of each day. In the morning, she'd read a few pages from one of the many spiritual quotation books that she kept by her bed, then she'd copy one she connected with onto a sheet of paper to carry with her. This would take between five and eight minutes each day. Before she left work in the evening, she'd read the quote again and ask to be guided to a place of centeredness and peacefulness.

Within three weeks, Amy's entire attitude changed. Her sleep improved, and so did her productivity at work, which she attributes to the slowing-down process that occurred through her newly formed rituals.

A RITUAL WITH BRACELETS

In my own life, the use of power bracelets has become a daily ritual that I've used for years to help me become more centered. Every morning, I take 11 individual bracelets, and one by one, put them on my left wrist. As I select each bracelet, I'll say a prayer acknowledging its meaning and asking for guidance in that area of my life. The 11 bracelets represent the following: the presence of angels, strength, love, financial independence, health and calmness, success in all areas, inspiration, power, creativity, manifesting my dreams, and spirituality. I also use a strand of mala beads, or Buddhist prayer beads, in much the same way. Similar to a rosary, I wrap this long series of beads around my wrist while saying prayers to begin my day.

This ritual helps me remember all that I want to become and allows me to stay connected to those intentions. Some people believe that the different stones the bracelets are made of have their own power to move us toward whatever they represent, such as rose quartz for love or tiger eye for creativity. Others believe that their power simply comes from our intention. While there may be truth to both of these claims, for me the real power comes from the slowing down required to perform this ritual. The whys and the hows aren't as important as finding a process that connects you with your spirit.

CANDLES AND CARD DECKS

Another technique I use to slow down is the lighting of candles. Prior to writing, I light a candle and ask for guidance in relating information that will help others and myself grow. Before each coaching session on the phone or in person, I perform the same ritual and ask for divine support. I suggest the same routine to clients who are looking for additional ways to prepare themselves for whatever task is at hand.

If you're feeling unsettled, here's another candle ritual you can use on a daily basis. Light several candles in your bathroom, fill the tub, and then shut off the lights and sit in silence (or put on some relaxing music). Then relax, breathe deeply, and ask for the guidance you desire. Repeat the words *relax* or *peace* as you sit surrounded by the soft, peaceful light that emanates from the candles around you. There's truly a calming effect that's achieved in a room with lit candles, and this simple, inexpensive ritual may be all that you need to do to help you slow down and find your connection to spirit.

Another popular way to slow down is through the use of various card decks that offer motivational quotes, Zen sayings, and positive expressions about money, angels, and more. Many of my clients place motivational cards on their desk at work to help them through stressful periods every day. And the great thing is, they work!

Since you become what you think about, why not carry a deck of these motivational cards with you? At the office, in your car, at school, or at home, these lightweight and inspirational messages can help you slow down, de-stress, and put yourself in a new state of mind. Take a deep breath, pull a card, and meditate on its meaning for a moment.

UNION WITH SPIRIT

As you can imagine, I still find myself seesawing back and forth in my own existence, one week staying on the path of awareness, and the next week slipping back into the fast-paced, mindless existence that disallows true union with spirit. I sometimes wonder how often I've missed opportunities to connect with God in my haste to accomplish all that needs to be done. Yet I've had some very powerful reminders of what can happen—even in the most unexpected places—when you slow down and connect with your center.

One time while on vacation in the Caribbean, I walked into a gift shop and was stopped in my tracks by a four-foot tall, three-foot-wide sculpture of Buddha. The hair on my arms raised, and I was drawn to the relic's beauty and the calm, peaceful expression on its face. Oh, to be in that place at all times! I continued to walk around the small art gallery in the back of the shop, but was once again drawn to this one beautiful piece of art.

What I found in that gift shop helped me connect with my source, and what transpired after the moving encounter with the Buddha statue was fantastic as well. When my companion and I returned to our room, we were immediately drawn to make love. But instead of rushing into it, we slowed down the process and just held each other for what seemed an eternity. When we finally did make love, it was incredible. A deep spiritual connectedness manifested itself in the act of sharing our hearts and bodies with each other.

I believe without a doubt that all of this was the result of our taking the time to explore the little gallery. I know that I don't have to travel thousands of miles to find a deeper connection to the spirit side of who I am, yet this experience opened my eyes to the need to live life at this slower pace. Had we not been open to walking into the shop, we would have missed the dazzling display of spiritual artifacts. It's through the process of slowing down that we get the chance to experience the real connectedness to our source, our core, our spirit. And when we offer the same to our partner through our physical bodies, we create a beautiful union on all levels.

Be on the lookout in your daily life for the five-minute exploration of the side road. Through the slowing down that comes with meditation and rituals, you can see a very rapid shift in how you experience the world.

※

Throughout the history of humankind, sages, saints, and successful people from all walks of life have enhanced their feeling of connectedness to the core of who they are through the daily use of meditation and rituals. I know that as you slow down, the same can happen to you! Get into the habit of doing your own ritual several times each day. It will give you a chance to pause, collect yourself, and live a more balanced life.

※ ※ ※

Part IV Review

As you learned in this section, living a centered life can help you become more at peace with yourself, and reaching this level of spiritual development may be as simple as adding a few minutes of prayer, meditation, or ritual to your daily routine.

Take a moment or two to slow down and review the information presented in Part IV. Remember that the writing exercises are truly the hidden gems of this work, and your written answers at the end of each part of this book will help you focus, create the intention to change, and then propel you forward as you set your action plan into motion.

The act of writing allows you to delve deeper into your mind to recall from the previous pages the information that was important to you and relevant to your life and desires. I believe that this is one of the many powerful steps that you can take in order to create the life you desire. So slow down, think, write, and then become who you truly want to be.

Please answer the following questions:

1. What was covered, in detail, in this section?

_____

_____

_____

_____

2. What was of most interest to you, and why?

_____

_____

_____

_____

3. What's the current plan of action you'll institute to help you achieve your goal? (Specifically list the steps you'll take to live the life
   you really want to.)

_____

_____

_____

_____

After you've answered these questions, move ahead to
Part V, where you'll build upon this connection with yourself and learn how to create the love you desire.

❊ ❊ ❊

PART V

to Create the

Love You Desire

chapter 10

The Path to Deep Love

One of the most honest love songs ever written, "You Can't Hurry Love," was turned into a smash hit by Diana Ross & The Supremes. Yet I have to wonder, how many of us truly follow this advice? Most of us are in a rush to find love because we think it will make us complete, but the cold, hard fact is that if we don't slow down enough to build an amazingly strong foundation within ourselves and then with another person, love will never last. The line in the song that talks about love not coming easy speaks of a reality that we don't always want to hear. We want the rush, the thrill, and the excitement . . . without the work it takes to deepen ourselves, communicate with a partner, and truly commit.

Throughout this chapter, I'll give you some examples of how you can slow down—regardless of whether you're single, dating, or married—so that you can truly feel the love within . . . and share it with another.

ARE YOU REALLY READY FOR LOVE?

Love demands that you honor the union between you and your partner so deeply that you're willing to let go of many of your own desires when that bond is threatened. Now, that's a hard pill for many people to swallow, but nonetheless it needs to be done if you want to create a lasting relationship. If you're not ready to put your own ego in the backseat at times so that your partner can go after his or her personal goals, then maybe you're not ready for love.

A number of years ago, a gentleman called my radio show with a comment on that day's topic, which was "How Do You Know When You're Ready for a Love Relationship?" His answer was short and to the point: "When you can allow your partner to pursue her life's dream, even if it means your dreams get put on hold, then you're ready for love." This man had been married two years and had just finished law school. An internship in Washington, D.C., had opened many doors for him—so many, in fact, that prestigious and lucrative job offers from respectable firms began to pour in weekly. His dream was being realized.

At the same time, his wife was applying for teaching positions around the country, since it was *her* dream to make a real difference in the lives of low-income children—kids who hadn't been given the best start in life. One day as the man sat reviewing a number of his own employment opportunities, his wife called. With tears of joy, she told him that she'd been offered the job she's always wanted—in one of the poorest sections of North Carolina. He remembered his vow to love and respect her for life, and decided never to mention his own prospects. Instead, he joined her in celebration and quickly moved to be by her side. He worked a variety of jobs for a few years until his wife decided that she was ready for a new challenge, at which time he told her about his career goals.

This man knew that his choice to support his wife created a bond that would never be broken. And now I'll ask you the same question that I ask myself: Are you willing to put your own desires on hold for a partner, as this man did?

BECOME THE PERSON YOU WANT TO BE WITH

Over the past ten years, many people have asked me, "How will I know when I'm ready for real love?" I often tell them that one of the first steps to finding love is to become the person they want to be with. So what kind of person do *you* want to love? Take a moment and write down at least ten characteristics or values of the type of person you want to fall in love with. (Some common answers might be: *honest, kind, vegetarian, passionate, someone who loves children, a thrill seeker* . . . I think you get the picture.)

1. _____

2. _____

3. _____

4. _____

5. _____

6. _____

7. _____

8. _____

9. _____

10. _____

Now slow down for a minute and be really honest with yourself. Of all of the traits you listed above, which ones do *you* need to work on the most? You see, when you become the person you want to meet, you're more likely to draw that person to you. If you live a chaotic lifestyle and want to be with someone who's calm, unless you begin to look for ways to relax yourself, you might just drive that person away.

I believe that while total opposites may be attracted to each other, when two individuals share many of their top-ten desired qualities, they often have a greater chance of enjoying a long-lasting union. The technique of defining these qualities on paper can really put single people on the fast track to finding a new partner and potential mate for life. Likewise, I've seen couples strengthen their relationships by slowing down, looking at the attributes their current mates have that they really love, and then trying to become more like that themselves. It's not as if you're trying to produce "mirror image" relationships here, because one person's definition of being "spiritual" or "spontaneous" or even "fit" can be totally different from someone else's. Just the act of slowing down and attempting to have more of the strong characteristics that you love in your partner can bring you both closer together.

EXAMINE YOUR INTENTION

A new client, Lisa, was frustrated because she still hadn't met the man of her dreams. She told me that she had everything else she wanted in life: a home, a great-paying job with benefits, and good health, yet she couldn't attract a potential long-term partner. So I asked her, "Why do you want to find this incredible man and get married?" She quickly responded, "David, I'm 38 and tired of doing everything on my own."

My next question led to an even deeper examination of her motives and why she might have been attracting the wrong types of guys into her life. I asked, "If you met the perfect man today—someone handsome, fit, emotionally stable, and so on—and he asked you the same question I just did, and you gave him the answer you gave me, 'I'm ready for love because I'm tired of doing everything on my own,' do you think he'd be ecstatic about falling in love with you?" In a matter of seconds, Lisa was laughing. "Well, I guess I'm not ready for the real thing yet," she admitted.

Through her weekly sessions with me and her journaling, Lisa realized that she needed to let go of her expectation that a man would "take care of everything." She also came to see how her belief that most men are not to be trusted was affecting her relationships. After all, thoughts create experiences, so if she believed that "men are dogs" and not trustworthy, might she be attracting men who fit this bill? And could she be driving good men away? Her new awareness led her to make some major changes in her life, and eventually, these changes helped her create a very healthy, happy relationship.

The success that Lisa experienced can be attributed to several factors: (1) Her desire to look honestly at her current and past beliefs and behaviors; (2) her willingness to work through her challenges by writing in her journal; and (3) her optimistic attitude, which allowed her to keep moving forward, even when it was painful to do so. In other words, Lisa was willing to slow down and uncover the facts about love and the role she had to play in order to invite it back into her life.

THE MYTHS OF MARRIAGE

A very difficult (and expensive) lesson that I had to learn—one that far too many of us figure out the hard way—is that marriage isn't the key to living a blissful life. Many of us still believe that once we've tied the knot, or once we've found our "soul mate," we'll be complete. We falsely assume that marriage is the end-all, the *coup de grâce*, the fantastic dessert in the meal called life. And if we hold on to these erroneous ideas, we'll surely see the divorce rate continue to rise.

Marriage can be an incredible experience, but only if we're truly ready for it. We need to pay attention to all that's going on in our current relationship and with our own expectations. It's only through this slowing down that we can uncover the myths, dismantle them, and then move forward into the sacred union of matrimony.

My personal experience taught me this lesson. I'd waited a long time to get married, and felt I was truly ready to commit all my heart and soul to the woman I was with. I was excited about the entire concept of our union, and I was ready to sacrifice my desires at times in order to serve my soon-to-be wife with love. I felt that we were moving to a sacred place, and I was finally comfortable enough with myself to offer all that I was to another person.

Unfortunately, the fantasy of marriage became all that I saw. I became so focused on being married that I blocked out all the serious problems we were experiencing. I didn't want to accept that this woman wasn't the person for me and that I wasn't the person for her, so I justified all the behaviors, actions, and beliefs she had that were screaming "She's not the one for you!" by telling myself that things would smooth out in the end. I didn't want to recognize that our core beliefs about love, life, money, and spirituality were simply incompatible. We just weren't right for each other.

Because I chose not to slow down (even after I had done this so well in many other areas of my life), I paid a very steep price. But relationships that don't last are experiences that we can learn and grow from, and this one offered some gems that can't be discarded. For starters, I was forced to reevaluate my perception of marriage and discard the fantasy that I, like many others, had created and held on to.

Again, the point is that when we slow down—and *only* when we slow down—we can look at life realistically and begin to make better and healthier decisions about love.

If you're single, divorced, or widowed, take a moment to answer the following questions:

- Are you ready for marriage today? Explain your answer.

- What myths about marriage do you carry with you?

_____

_____

_____

_____

- What can you do today for you own growth to increase your chances of having a healthy marriage?

_____

_____

_____

_____

- Why do you think most marriages fail?

_____

_____

_____

_____

Slow down for marriage. Remember, love relationships are meant to enable a couple to create an existence that allows them the satisfaction of retaining their individuality, while at the same time knowing that there's something much bigger that they share together.

CAN YOU LIVE WITH EACH OTHER?

I remember being at a wedding once where I got into a wonderful discussion with a 74-year-old man about love and marriage. He'd been married for 50 years, and was saddened that all his children had been divorced several times. When I asked him why he thought the divorce rate was so high, his answer surprised me: "You can fall in love with a thousand people over your lifetime," he said, "but you'll only be able to live with a tiny fraction of that number seven days a week." *Words of wisdom*, I thought.

The man went on to say that over the years, he and his wife had traveled all over the country with their friends, and while he found several of the women who went on these trips very attractive, after spending one or two days in a hotel with them and their husbands, he always knew that he had chosen his partner perfectly. He couldn't have lived with any of the other women, but he and his wife worked together beautifully.

Slow down and think about how important this concept is: You may love someone deeply, yet if you can't live with them, how will your marriage last?

I once knew a couple that experienced this firsthand. The wife would tell her husband over and over how much she cherished him, and how her love for him was more important than any material possessions, yet she restricted his involvement in decorating their home. Since he was a very creative person, he would periodically offer suggestions about the look of their place, but her response was cold and hurtful. She let him know that she thought this was the responsibility of the wife, and that his role was to leave these projects up to her. She even chastised him several times for bringing home "ridiculous" pieces of art that didn't match her decor.

The husband was confused: On the one hand, his wife was telling him that she loved him more than any material possession, yet on the other, she was making it quite clear that his input didn't matter. He couldn't stand being treated this way, and eventually, even though her loved her very much, he decided that this was not a match.

WHEN SHOULD YOU MARRY?

I once got a call from a 20-year-old girl who asked for my support. She wanted to marry her 22-year-old lover of two years, but her family was dead set against such a thing, even though she knew he was "the one." "If he's 'the one,'" I asked, "will he still be around in one, two, or five years?" This was a question she didn't want to hear. "Yes, but we're so in love that we want to do it now," she replied. "There's no point in waiting."

I told her that I'm a big fan of marriage, and even though I'm a liberal thinker, I'm also in favor of the traditional roles that a husband and wife take on once they consummate their relationship. (In a way it's an oxymoron, isn't it—a liberal thinker with a love of traditional roles?) Anyway, I shot straight with her and said that I didn't think many couples under the age of 30 have much chance of making a marriage work in the societal structure we live in today. Before I could go on, she decided that she'd heard enough and hung up the phone. She had envisioned, I'm sure, quite a different answer from a guy who over the years seemed to promote all kinds of risk taking to get ahead and really experience life. But when it comes to age and marriage, I have a totally different outlook.

I believe that men should wait until they're at least 30 years old before they marry. It takes most men this long to reach the level of maturity needed to give their marriage the best possible chance of making it. They also need this time to select a career, get established, and become a man. I do know guys who marry younger than this and make it, but I believe that the odds are definitely in favor of those who wait. And judging by the enormous response that I received about this topic on my former radio show, most people see this as a very wise wait indeed.

I also believe that women should wait until they're at least 25 before marrying, since they tend to reach a level of maturity that can handle the responsibility of marriage much sooner than men do. However, I still say *wait*—no one should enter into this serious a commitment until they've had a chance to experience the ups and downs of life. There's nothing—no seminar, no book, and no amount of education—that can take the place of life experience.

Both men and women should seriously date at least four partners before they say "I do." In a way, this practice helps you decide what type of partner you really want to be with. Doing so will allow you to discern not only the type of person you can truly connect with at a deep level, but it also lets you see more deeply into who you are as a person. If you're open, you'll recognize the parts of yourself that you need to work on to create the best you possible.

Now, once you've found the right person to marry (at the right time, of course), wouldn't it be nice if someone, somewhere, found a formula that would guarantee the success of your union? I don't have any such magic, but I can offer some general guidance that can give your relationship an edge when you're experiencing challenging times:

- Respect and communication between two people can lead to a feeling of safety, which is essential for any lasting marriage.

- The desire to serve one's partner is critical, as is the need for some type of compatible spiritual belief.

- It's extremely important that couples come to an agreement to try to help each other feel that they're part of a team, with general goals regarding family life as well as discussions around individual growth within the union.

- It's also necessary to discuss financial goals, expenses, and savings plans, as well as the true financial situation that each individual is in. No surprises are appreciated after the wedding, where one partner has misrepresented his or her income or withheld important information about current debt. (If you've been in either of these positions, then you know how trust is immediately threatened due to the withholding of such details.)

BE OPEN TO LOVE—NO MATTER WHAT

One of the most exciting programs I ever had on my radio show had to do with the dilemma many individuals face when they're involved with people much older or younger than they are. These folks are bombarded with all kinds of advice from well-meaning friends and family members—from "He's old enough to be your father!" to "How could you marry someone 20 years younger than you?" Yet those who called my show who were involved in marriages like this couldn't have been more enthusiastic about their choices. By my estimate, at least 90 percent of these individuals had found success in a marriage where the age difference between the partners ranged from 11 to 20 years, and in most of these cases, they didn't think early on that the age difference would help or hinder their relationship; they were simply open to love without their own self-imposed limitations.

What makes these marriages work is that in each of them, both partners found a mate who had very similar beliefs about the key topics I've already mentioned: communication, honesty, spiritual practices, finances, and so on. Those who married someone younger were often drawn to the energy and open-mindedness that their partner brought to their life; while many of those who married someone quite older fell in love with the wisdom and patience that the other person exhibited. And yes, most had never guessed that they would have become involved in this type of relationship—much less that it would lead to marriage.

When we refuse to open ourselves up to the romantic possibilities we've never considered, we may be missing out on the partner who could be the lost piece to our life puzzle. I think we do ourselves a great disservice by automatically saying, "That would never work for me," until we've explored the option more thoroughly. In other words, never automatically exclude any possibilities. Instead, slow down and challenge the status quo. Look for love and marriage in what might seem to be the most unlikely places, for that's where you just might find it. If only for a moment, release your stereotypical beliefs that say your life partner must look a certain way or make a particular amount of money or be in a specific age group. Slow down for love.

❋ ❋ ❋

chapter 11

The Red Flags and Healthy Boundaries of Love

The only way to stop repeating past relationship errors is to slow down and examine them. We all know about "relationship red flags," but when we get caught up in the fairy tale of love, we don't always want to be honest with ourselves and others about any trouble spots we may see.

The following is a list of some mistakes that can potentially block real love. Do any of them apply to you?

- Saying "I love you" too quickly.

- Becoming physically intimate before you truly know the other person and his or her intentions and desires.

- Not knowing what you truly want out of a love relationship—that is, are you seeking a serious commitment, or are you at a point where you just want to date?

Next is a list of relationship red flags. Do you ever find
yourself ignoring these warning signs?

- You feel that if you found your soul mate, life
  would be fantastic.

- You're afraid to voice your own opinions in a
  new relationship.

- You go along with the your partner's wishes,
  even when you'd normally say, "No, thank
  you."

- When you enter new relationships, you drop
  out of sight from your friends and put your
  usual activities on hold.

- New relationships make you feel afraid to
  trust your feelings and speak to your partner
  about them.

- You're still looking for your "knight" or
  "princess."

This whole slowing-down process is about becoming
more aware of who you are, the strengths you have, and the
personal challenges you have to overcome to bring true
love into your life. After all, if you refuse to slow down and
look at your past errors, how do you expect to avoid repeating them?

Take some time right now to write about poor choices
or judgments you've made in previous relationships (you
know, the ones that you don't want to repeat and that you

know can't be a part of a healthy future). Please do this now before reading any further, as this exercise can help you take a huge leap forward and set yourself up for success.

_____

_____

_____

_____

_____

_____

Now review your list of past relationship mistakes. You may not feel comfortable seeing this in black and white, but that's the purpose of this exercise. In fact, one of the reasons I don't believe in "talk-only" therapy is that when your red flags are staring at you from a piece of paper, they really hit home. So please follow this process because it works.

SETTING HEALTHY BOUNDARIES

Some people feel that they have so much love to give to a partner that if they don't offer it to another person immediately, it will be wasted. They may think, *If only I had someone to shower with this unused passion, that person would benefit immensely, and I'd finally feel alive!* But the truth is that when one partner shows the other so much affection that it feels smothering, the other person may enjoy it for a brief period, but then he or she will probably feel overwhelmed and start to retreat. On the flip side, if the one who's giving all the adulation doesn't start getting something back in return, he or she will begin to resent it, too. Soon, both people end up feeling manipulated and used, and the relationship dies.

One of the personal challenges I faced many years ago was being up front with people I dated and setting healthy boundaries. If I was casually dating someone who told me that they loved me, I felt I had to commit and be with that person exclusively. I didn't have the courage to say, "I'm so grateful that you feel so strongly, and thank you." I usually felt obligated to return those precious words, regardless of whether or not I meant them. That would often lead to physical intimacy, and each of us moving way too quickly without talking about what we wanted in life and what we expected from each other. The "penned in" feeling that I would then get came from my fear of hurting the other person if I wasn't at the same place romantically.

After years of painful breakups and hurt feelings, I finally got to the place where I could speak honestly about my feelings. Since I was in the healthy-dating phase of my life, I would explain to my partners that while I found them very attractive and fun to be with, I couldn't promise anything more than a casual relationship. Some women were very open to where I was, while others were looking for a long-term commitment and decided to move on. Either way, everyone was on the same page, and that honesty led me to a beautiful new path of living and speaking from my heart. I'm just sorry it took me so long to get to the point where I was willing to let a wonderful potential dating partner go if she was looking for a more exclusive relationship.

As I learned, being honest and establishing healthy boundaries is essential to creating lasting love. Here are a few to tips to help you do just that:

- Hold off on making love with someone until you know yourself, your desires, and where you truly are in life and are able to state this clearly, even if it means the other person may be unhappy or walk away. The same goes for the other person.

- If you think your relationship is headed for premature physical intimacy, discuss alternatives to lovemaking where both you and your partner can give and receive affection. Stay true to this path, even though the temptation to make love may remain present. If you know you can't hold back your desire when it's in your best interests to do so, then don't put yourself in a situation where you may break your healthy boundaries.

- If something seems "off" in your relationship, ask your partner for some time to discuss your feelings. Very often your gut feelings are right on, even if you have no tangible proof that something is amiss. Setting up a strong line of communication early in a relationship will help build a foundation for this or any future relationship you have.

- Continue developing your own interests and activities. Although you may initially want to be with your love interest 24/7, setting healthy boundaries will help you keep your own life in line. When you put everything on hold for another person—workouts, your meditation or prayer time, or your relationships with friends—you're headed down the road to resentment.

Slowing down and setting these types of boundaries may sound like work, and maybe it is. But these steps will allow you to finally move toward creating the kind of relationship you desire. Remember, knowing what you want and being honest about your needs allows you to respect yourself and your partner.

JOHN'S STORY

Many very intelligent people simply dismiss the red flags that pop up all around them until it's too late. John's story is no different. "She seems like the perfect partner," he told me at our first session. "She's intelligent, attractive, successful in business . . ." and the accolades went on. John met this woman the previous year at a business function and had been immediately taken by her good looks. She'd flirted with him, making it quite clear that she was interested in him as well. They set a date for lunch, but then she admitted that she was seriously involved with another man. John decided not to pursue the relationship until eight months later, when he got an unexpected phone call at his office from this same woman, who was now single and interested in getting together with him as soon as possible.

Within the first week of dating, it had become a rather intense love affair. By day eight, she was requesting that he spend five or more nights a week at her house, even though she had two children whom John barely knew. Nevertheless, he began to spend more and more time with her, and he even began to feel bad on the nights he had to leave. On these occasions, she would tell him she loved him and literally beg him to stay.

At first it was flattering, but soon John started feeling smothered. He wondered how she could know so quickly that she loved him, but he never talked to her about his reservations. In the meantime, spending so much time at this woman's house was cutting into the downtime he needed to recoup his energy and relax from his high-pressure job, and he began to resent her neediness—but he still felt too guilty to tell her.

Other things began to happen that concerned John as well—such as the 2 A.M. phone calls that his new girlfriend didn't want to talk about, other than to say that they were from an old friend. As the weeks went by, her neediness seemed to increase, as did the phone calls at odd hours, and John realized that he'd never asked her about her last relationship—why it ended, how it ended, or if it had actually ended at all.

From an outside vantage point, I was able to see very clearly what was going on. So my questions to John began to center on the aspects of what a healthy relationship looked like. I asked him if in a healthy relationship, a person would:

- be so quick to ask someone to sleep over when he or she has two small children at home;

- refuse to discuss frequent phone calls at all hours of the night;

- avoid talking about prior relationships; or

- exhibit such "needy" behavior as having to have a lover around so often, and so soon after a breakup?

John saw quite quickly that the answers to all these questions were a big no, yet he still couldn't bring himself to approach his girlfriend and speak honestly about what was troubling him. It really shouldn't have come as a surprise when a few weeks later, she called him at the office to tell him that she couldn't see him anymore, because she'd started seeing her ex-boyfriend again.

John saw it all coming way before it hit him, and he was really frustrated with himself for not paying close enough attention to all the warning signs he'd gotten. He, like so many others, found out that in love, you need to heed the wisdom within, the feeling in your stomach that screams, "Warning!" This experience was an incredible learning opportunity, one that he grew from immensely.

DROP THE SCORECARD

Do you constantly keep score in your relationship? Do you always need to win? I remember doing an interview with best-selling author Wayne Dyer a number of years ago, when he made a statement about relationships that I'll never forget. We were discussing the keys to long-lasting love when he remarked, "David, we always have the choice to be right or be kind." I haven't always followed this great advice, and there have been times when I've been caught up in an "I'm right and you're wrong" situation. One of the poems from my book *Phoenix Soul: One Man's Search for Love and Inner Peace* reflects this idea. It's called "Respect":

How many times have relationships crumbled
Because neither side could let go of false pride
To respect
Leave the fight early
All battles end with one combatant left

Keeping score in any relationship will eventually weaken the union. Even if you're not the type of person who has to win every argument, there may be other ways that you undermine your bond—perhaps, for instance, by keeping a mental tally of what your partner does for you compared to what you do for your him or her. Unfortunately, it's human nature to do this, and many of us aren't aware of how damaging this practice can be.

The fact is that in a healthy relationship, there will be times where you may, in truth, be doing more than your "fair share" to keep the relationship moving forward, but that's just life. If you find yourself saying, "I called him the last three times, so if he wants to talk, he can call me," or "I've made dinner and cleaned out the cat box every night this week, so if she wants to eat, she can cook something herself," know that this score keeping will surely lead to more resentment. Is that what you really want?

Next time, instead of pulling out your mental scorecard, express your concerns with love. Voice your thoughts from a positive perspective, highlighting what your partner does that makes you feel great instead of holding a grudge and simmering inside. For example, if you feel as if you're the one making all the effort to communicate, you might say, "Honey, I love it when you surprise me by calling me at work. It really makes me feel loved."

We need to realize that a perfect balance in any aspect of life is impossible. Let go of the need for your lover to respond with three straight surprise phone calls to even the score. Keep leading by example, and your relationship is sure to benefit.

FINDING YOUR SOUL MATE

Over the years, I've had the chance to interview dozens of spiritual writers, philosophers, and sex therapists about what it takes to create the unbreakable loving bond with another that so many of us search for. None of these interviews, though, has been more colorful than the one I did with sex therapist and author Barbara Keesling, Ph.D. Known for her expertise in all areas of sexual techniques, Barbara totally took me by surprise one day when we were discussing the most important aspects of a love relationship.

She said, "Without a doubt, the most important component of deep love is that there be a connection on the soul level. When people ask me what my favorite position in sex is, I always say, 'A philosophical one.' Everything else is just window dressing. The various techniques, positions, and paraphernalia . . . while I'm a big fan of all of that stuff, the real key is that two people connect and feel for each other from the soul."

I was surprised and happy to hear Barbara say this, because it seems to me that too many people decide that a certain person is the one for them because they're physically attracted to each other, or they have a good friendship. They don't even question whether a deeper connection is needed for a relationship to endure, or perhaps they've just given up on finding it. I remember one exasperated caller from San Francisco who, after another relationship had just fizzled before her eyes, asked, "How will I know when I've found my soul mate?" My answer may seem elementary, yet it's the truth: If you slow down, trust yourself, and take the time to work on your own imperfections, you'll know the difference between someone you should just date and learn from and the individual you should commit your life to.

The more you trust, follow, and act upon your intuition, the easier it is to find lasting love. Your intuitive side is the part of you that says, "Red flags ahead!" or "This person is the one." So, in essence, as simple as it may seem, when you slow down, it becomes easier to discern whether or not you have a soul connection with someone.

Examine this topic for yourself right now. What does it mean to have a deeper soul connection? How would you feel if you had one? What would this type of relationship look like? Slow down, take a moment, and write out the answers to these questions below. Your answers will help you evaluate your relationships now and in the future.

_____

_____

_____

_____

_____

Feel Safe

ling of safety is the difference between a good
onship and a great soul connection. If there was
one   ale sign that spelled success for a partnership, it
would be this feeling. And while your perception of safety
can grow and deepen over time, it's usually something that's
evident from the very beginning.

Feeling safe allows you to be who you are with the person you love, without the fear that you're not enough, or that you must somehow change to win their respect. It allows you to share your greatest dreams or deepest insecurities and know that you won't be laughed at or thought of as silly—and you can rest assured that whatever you tell your partner won't be used as a tool to hurt you later on.

In any relationship, feeling safe needs to be a two-way street. When you share intimate information, be sure that your partner also feels comfortable discussing dreams and fears as well. Unfortunately, I've seen too many relationships crumble because only one partner took the risk to be open, honest, and vulnerable. While initially it may feel good to be with someone who's always willing to listen, be wary if that person isn't sharing his or her innermost thoughts and feelings as well. That's a real sign of trouble ahead, because a "nondisclosing" partner may be unwilling to risk being real, which means that you're not on equal footing in the relationship. Take this as a warning, similar to the one issued by police officers across America: "Whatever you say can and will be used against you."

A therapist called in to my program once to share his opinions on the topic of feeling safe. He explained that some people, either consciously or subconsciously, will "lure" their partner into a false sense of safety in order to try to gain the upper hand in a relationship. They'll encourage their partner to bare their soul to them, and will always be willing to listen intently to their lover's dreams and insecurities. While all this sounds fine at first, what the vulnerable ones don't realize is that their partners have actually shared very little, if any, of their own fears, insecurities, or vulnerabilities. This makes the listeners feel in control, and down the road these people may look for ways to use the private information shared with them by their lovers as a weapon. What a sad way to be in a relationship.

However, when two people are striving for real love, none of these games occur. In a caring relationship, neither partner would purposely bring up shared secrets during a disagreement in order to control or hurt the other, because they would realize that the damage this can cause may be irreversible. Healthy relationships are those in which both partners talk honestly about their past experiences in love, current financial situations, future hopes and dreams, and even spiritual experiences without the fear that these expressions could ever be used against them.

FINAL THOUGHTS ON SLOWING DOWN TO FIND LOVE

Love follows no guidelines and has no set path—it just appears. On the wings of the mourning dove, it flies into your life one day, without warning. When you fall in love, you simply respond to the call of your soul.

Love brings with it no promise that the road will always be smooth, without curves or fallen trees. Remember: Just because you're on the right path doesn't mean it's the easiest one, but love will offer you comfort in any storm, if you're willing to wait it out.

At times, your soul mate may bring you to places that you'd rather not visit. Go there anyway, and shine a light in all the nooks and crannies of your unexplored heart that you'd rather not see, feel, or acknowledge. Your lover may expose you to parts of yourself that you're insecure about, parts you don't like, even parts that seem unlovable, but in doing so will help you heal, grow, and eventually love your entire being. To be completely loved is to be completely free, and to love completely is to look at your partner without contempt for his or her imperfections.

I know that the most incredible experiences I've had in my life have all been centered around love—as they should be. When you slow down and see the love that you already are, you will be on your way to finally experiencing all that you could possibly be.

❋ ❋ ❋

Part V Review

Creating the love you desire with yourself and others is a never-ending and exciting process, one that can only begin if you slow down and look at your current beliefs and actions as you have in this section.

Take a moment or two to slow down and review the information presented in Part V. Remember that the writing exercises are truly the hidden gems of this work, and your written answers at the end of each part of this book will help you focus, create the intention to change, and then propel you forward as you set your action plan into motion.

The act of writing allows you to delve deeper into your mind to recall from the previous pages the information that was important to you and relevant to your life and desires. I believe that this is one of the many powerful steps that you can take in order to create the life you desire. So slow down, think, write, and then become who you truly want to be.

Please answer the following questions:

1. What was covered, in detail, in this section?

_____

_____

_____

_____

2. What was of most interest to you, and why?

_____

_____

_____

_____

3. What's the current plan of action you'll institute to help you achieve your goal? (Specifically list the steps you'll take to live the life you really want to.)

_____

_____

_____

_____

After you've answered these questions, move ahead to Part VI, where you'll examine the ways in which you can serve the world and yourself.

❋ ❋ ❋

PART VI

Slow Down

to Serve the World
and Yourself

chapter 12

Serving Yourself
and Others

I believe with all my heart that every success we achieve is linked somehow, in some way, to serving others. When we use our talents, empathy, patience, passion, sensitivity, and compassion to look for ways to make someone else's day easier—when "What can we *do for* the world?" replaces "What can we *get from* the world?"—we create a powerful aura around us that leads to a greater amount of joy and connectedness.

When we're out of the habit of serving, we may have to begin by consciously reminding ourselves to be on the lookout for opportunities to help others. For example, we can open doors for strangers, pick up litter in our neighborhoods, let other commuters merge ahead of us in traffic, or even send a card to a friend we haven't seen for a while. While cultivating the service attitude must begin as a conscious decision, after a period of time it just becomes who we are.

Here's what Mahatma Gandhi had to say on the subject: "He who devotes himself to service with a clear conscience will day by day grasp the necessity for it in greater measure, and will continually grow richer in faith. Consciously or unconsciously, every one of us does render some service or another. If we cultivate the habit of doing this service deliberately, our desire for service will steadily grow stronger, and will make not only for our own happiness, but that of the world at large." [*The Words of Gandhi*, Newmarket Press]

So how did you serve others at home, at work, or in your neighborhood today? Write your answer below.

_____

_____

_____

_____

Without knowing that this question was coming, were you able to find one or more ways that you consciously served the people you encountered this day? If you couldn't recall any particular incidents, there's no need to worry or feel guilty. You can't begin to change unless you know where you currently are, so take a few moments right now to think about how you can do more to serve.

THE BENEFITS OF SERVICE

The benefits you receive when you decide to focus on other people are quite incredible. You become emotionally stronger, you feel more joy in everyday activities, your self-confidence and self-esteem grow, and your energy level rises as you feel better about yourself and the reason for your existence. And once you see that helping others is one of the main reasons for your being here on Earth, it turns into a spiritual experience.

The joy on the faces of people who have committed their lives to fulfilling the needs of others is unmistakable. Their laughter is real and from the heart, and their smiles are authentic. Just think of the Dalai Lama and Mother Teresa—or maybe you can remember a former teacher or a neighbor who had this glow around them. That energy is unmistakably one of the miraculous benefits that comes to those who dedicate their lives to those around them.

The great thing about service is that it doesn't take much to really make a difference in someone else's day. I once worked with a client named Diane who had just lost her job and was stressed to the max, yet she'd decided to commit to serving the world through her daily actions. During one of our sessions, despite her determination to break her habit of pessimistic thinking, she had a hard time keeping her composure, and her tears flowed freely. She later told me that on her way home, she saw a dump truck trying to merge into her lane. Numerous other cars refused to let the truck in, and it became stuck in the intersection. Diane said that she normally would have blown by the truck, but instead she stayed focused on her desire to serve and let the driver get ahead of her—even though he was moving at an excruciatingly slow speed. The dump-truck driver honked and waved several times, showing his sincere appreciation for her courtesy, and somehow, through this act, a glimpse of joy came into Diane's life.

Diane ended up getting stuck at another red light, where she proceeded to call and leave me a message proclaiming her victory. She saw that even in her pain, this simple gesture had left a warm feeling in her heart.

So what are the benefits that come with service? People who choose this lifestyle become more energized, joyful, confident, emotionally balanced, connected to life, and at peace with who they are. And these are just a few characteristics, for there are many other individual transformations that occur in people who shift their attention from themselves to others. For instance, these individuals begin to draw caring people to them who naturally assist each other along their career paths and with their personal goals. These types of people, if they're single, also begin to bring in to their inner circle others who can introduce them to like-minded individuals to date. Once you become entrenched in this way of living, you'll have a built-in support team to help lift you out of the personal ruts you may fall into from time to time.

GIVE WHAT YOU WANT TO RECEIVE

Many years ago, if someone had told me that all I had to do to get what I wanted out of life was to *give* more of what I desired, I wouldn't have understood the power behind this philosophy. I might have even posed the following questions:

- If I want more money and have so little, how can I give any of it away?

- If I desire deep love and I'm in a lousy relationship, how can I be expected to give more to the person I'm with?

- If I'm single, how do I give love if there's no one with me?

- If I want a great job and I'm in one I despise, what sense does it make to work harder?

While on the surface these questions seem to make sense, we have to remember that we get what we put into something, and every success we achieve in life will be linked in one way or another to what we do for other people.

During one of my interviews with author Deepak Chopra, M.D., he explained this principle using the example of creating great wealth. He said that money needs to circulate, like the blood in our body. If we hold on to it for fear that we'll never have enough, it's like putting a tourniquet on an artery, and we'll stop the flow of money into our lives. But if we serve the world with our money—even though at times it may be in short supply—then we'll be rewarded in kind.

So if, for example, you want more money, then give it away to someone who needs it more than you do, or to a person or organization that helps you stay focused, centered, and balanced. I remember meeting a woman who was truly committed to writing a book to help people along their spiritual path. She wanted to print her work through a print-on-demand publisher, but didn't have the money to do so. I loved the energy she had for this dream and sent her a check to help her on her way. Even though times were financially tough for me at that moment, I showed no fear of lack—to me, the opportunity to serve her was a great chance to prove that I was living the life I believed in. Just two weeks after sending this woman the money, an unexpected check came to me for 20 times what I'd sent to her. This principle works!

In keeping with the previous example, please slow down and answer these questions:

- How can you serve others today with the finances you currently have?

_____

_____

- What percentage of your weekly income are you willing to share?

_____

_____

- Whom will you give your next donation to, and on what date?

_____

_____

GETTING THE JOB YOU WANT BY SERVING OTHERS

Jim was a client of mine from the Midwest who was looking for a new career path. He'd just found out that he had an interview for a sales positions with a large company, and he was very excited. That was the good news. The bad news? He was up against 300 other applicants!

I asked Jim to focus his energies on developing a service-oriented mentality. "Who would a supervisor be the most impressed with?" I asked him. "An applicant bent on helping the company grow and exceed its goals, or someone who just wanted a job?" I suggested that what would set him apart from all the other prospective employees was if he was the only one asking his potential boss how he could be of most service to the company.

Jim and I came up with a list of questions that he planned to ask during the interview. They went something like this:

- Is there anything that you'd like to see me accomplish that the last person in this position wasn't able to do?

- How can I most efficiently help this division reach and exceed all of its goals?

- How can I serve you and your needs through my position?

- What did the last person who held his position do well that you'd like to see continued?

- What else can I do to strengthen my skills if I'm hired for this job?

I would have loved to have seen the look on the interviewer's face as Todd rattled off his list of service-oriented questions. As you may have guessed, Todd got the job—he beat out all the other applicants by putting the company's needs ahead of his own. But imagine what the outcome of the interview might have been had Todd asked these typical questions instead:

- What's the starting salary?

- What does it take to get a raise?

- How many vacation days do I get?

Too often we forget about the importance of service during our job search. If we'd slow down and think about the type of person *we'd* want to hire, we'd surely prepare for interviews differently. As a matter of fact, we'd do just as Todd did.

I remember reading an article about Ben Wallace, a professional basketball player. He was passed over in the NBA draft out of college, so he decided to take an opportunity to play for a foreign-league team, hoping that it would lead to a chance to play professionally in the U.S. Shortly thereafter, he was invited to try out for the Washington Wizards, and the coaches were so impressed with his intense hustle that they signed him on. At 6'9" and 240 pounds, he was running the court like a point guard on every play. They said that he had great athletic talent, but his basketball skills needed work. In the end, what really got them enthused about his future was how he went all out, giving 110 percent whenever he was on the floor. A few years later, Ben signed a $30 million contract with the Detroit Pistons. He knew how to serve.

So where do you stand with respect to your career goals? Are you doing what you love? Do you feel satisfied? Are you still stuck, wondering why opportunities seem to be passing you by? Slow down, for success in life is all about service—it takes a desire to consciously *serve* more, to achieve more.

Whether you're actively searching for a new job or looking for advancement at the one you already have, taking a few moments to answer the following questions will help you prepare for your next step.

- If you're going on a job interview soon, what types of service-related questions should you ask the interviewer?

_____

_____

_____

_____

- At your current job, how can you serve your supervisor more efficiently? How can you help the company you work for accomplish its most important objectives? If you own your own business, how can you better support your associates and help them contribute to your company's mission?

_____

_____

_____

_____

- How can you serve your co-workers more
  effectively? How can you help them accomplish their goals?

- What can you do outside of your current job
  to help guarantee your future success?

When you adopt the service mentality, you'll never lose.
Even if the job or promotion you really want doesn't become
available to you, you will still have gained the experience,
wisdom, and knowledge that will open new doors for you
down the road. You'll move yourself up to the "5 Percent
Club," the place where the top achievers are. And while 95
percent of people are whining or complaining about how life
isn't fair and they never get the breaks, you'll be guarantee-
ing your future success.

(As an aside, the principle of service also applies to employers. A friend of mine, attorney Jeffrey Meldon, has a large and devoted staff—a very committed group of people whom *he* serves on a daily basis, even though according to a business "depth chart," they're all "underneath" him. His motivational audio library at work continues to grow and grow at his expense as he encourages them to take time to develop personally. And not only does he regularly stock this great audio library, but he actually pays his employees a bonus when they finish any of the available cassettes. By doing so, he continues to attract the most motivated people to work for him.)

SERVE WITH LOVE TO RECEIVE LOVE

In healthy relationships, it's second nature to look for ways to make sure your lover's needs are being met on a daily basis. In fact, the growth and success of the partnership depends on the conscious act of service. But what if you're in a relationship that has stalled? The fact is that if there's any chance at all for you to get the love you desire, you need to keep giving it out as long as you choose to stay with your mate.

Serving a partner in a love relationship that has soured is never easy, but it's really the only way to go if you want to salvage the union. What other option do you honestly have? If you cut love off in one direction, don't you also block the flow of love back to you? (Keep in mind Dr. Chopra's example of the tourniquet on the artery.)

I discovered the truth of this principle for myself years ago. I was really struggling in a relationship, and after a long, drawn-out argument with my partner that consisted of nothing more than "I'm right, and you're wrong" accusations, I went for a drive to clear my head. While in the car, I called a counselor and asked for her opinion. She immediately told me that I knew exactly what I had to do, and even if it was hard, it was my only option. I knew what she meant: I had to serve, and I needed to show my partner love, even though—trust me—it was the last thing I wanted to do.

I went back home, and for the next three days I decided not to argue with my lover, regardless of what happened. Even though she was unresponsive to my efforts during this period of time, I continued to kiss her on the forehead every morning as I got out of bed. During the day, I'd periodically give her a hug, even though she usually just walked away.

I knew I'd played a definite role in the upheaval of our relationship, so I did my best to rise above my feelings and serve her—and *us*—in whatever way I could. While in the end these attempts didn't salvage our relationship, they did teach me a powerful lesson: I could continue to give affection even though I wasn't immediately receiving it back. This served as a powerful personal reminder that I was worthy of a more loving relationship than the one I was currently in.

It's easy to come to a stalemate, to say it's someone else's fault and that they're the ones who need to change or apologize. Yet even if you're right (although being 100 percent right in a relationship struggle rarely occurs), how will you possibly get love if you're not willing to give it?

To get all that you desire in love, serve your partner. Or, if you're single, look for ways to serve in other relationships. That might mean being a better friend or a great listener, or learning techniques to help you become more patient. When you do so, you prepare yourself for love. If you've done your best to be loving and caring toward your current partner and the relationship doesn't last, your healthy and powerful attitude will carry you forward into the next relationship. There, you'll both benefit from the beautiful fruits of your labor.

Please slow down and answer the following questions:

- How have you served your partner today?

_____

_____

_____

_____

- What can you do tomorrow, regardless of your current relationship situation, to bring love into your life through service?

_____

_____

_____

_____

- What can you do to serve your partner when your relationship is being challenged?

_____

_____

_____

_____

When you come to realize that the only way to get what you really want is to give that very same thing, you'll truly understand the power of serving.

❀ ❀ ❀

chapter 13

Let Go of the End Result to Get Everything You Want and Need

There's an approach to life that says to be successful you must "get focused, set a plan, work relentlessly every day, never say never, put your blinders on, pull your bootstraps up, and work, work, and work some more. Never let go of the specific goal you've set! Go, go, go!" I once fell victim to living in this manner, and while it worked some of the time, it usually set me up for such disappointment that I knew I had to find a better way. And I have. I've discovered that if I want more money, a better career, deeper love, or better health, I need to set my goal, and then *let go of my need to have it come out the way I think it should.* In other words, I must let go of the end result.

Many people may be wondering why I'd recommend such a thing. After all, haven't we been taught that the reason we set goals and go after them with gusto is to *attain* them? Isn't that what "successful" people do? The fact is that this old mind-set is what creates stress, and it leads to frustration and unhappiness.

Allow me to explain. What if you fall in love with someone and set a goal that says you *have* to be with him or her,

could possibly satisfy you, and that this per-
and only soul mate—and then it doesn't work
imagine the emotional impact that this could
In this scenario, it's easy to see why some
people take years to get over a lost relationship, while others may never recover enough to be open to real love again.

Here's another example: What about that "perfect" job—the one that you're certain will finally transform your life into something meaningful? What if you set goals, work hard, go to school, and sacrifice your friendships and love relationships for that perfect position . . . and then you never get it? Or you *do* get it, but it falls short of your expectations? The disappointment might be enough to throw you into a tailspin, and your resentment of the hours spent day after day in the "dream job" that you now despise could open the door to addiction, weight gain, and stress, robbing you of joy.

Now imagine that you've accepted the powerful philosophy of letting go of the outcome you imagine. If you tell yourself, "I will go after my dreams with all my energy, but I release my need for things to work out as I envision—I let go of the end result," do you see how this keeps you open to change along the way? Even though you may want one thing today, you're keeping yourself open to the possibility that there may be a different or better option available to you down the road. If you're stuck in the old "blind model" of success, you may not ever even see these opportunities when they present themselves.

When we become so attached to the outcome of any goal that we begin to lose touch with who we are, what our beliefs and needs are, and why we're going after a certain goal in the first place, then negativity, blame, and bitterness begin to creep into our existence. For instance, I once knew a single mother who wanted nothing more than to be financially secure. She was sure that this would make her happy, so she worked hard for years and finally got the break she was waiting for: a large salary with lots of perks. The catch was that her new job often took her away from her home and her child. And because she was so focused on having more money (erroneously believing that it would bring her happiness), she lost herself in the process as well. She became negative and bitter toward her career and the travel that kept her on the road, but she wouldn't give it up. She'd attached herself so strongly to the end result she desired that she wouldn't change in order to restore her happiness. Consequently, she lost many love relationships and saw her child infrequently as she continued to chase the almighty dollar.

Learn from this woman's example: Slow down and let go of the end result before it's too late for you, too.

❋

Now, please understand that letting go doesn't mean giving up. For example, as a kid, my idea of a successful day of fishing was one in which we caught fish—lots of them. Over the years, I've totally released the need for that to occur. When I fish today, my joy comes from being outdoors and enjoying the oceans, lakes, and streams that offer such beauty to our world. And even if I don't catch a thing, I see the day as supremely successful.

Likewise, one of my clients recently applied for a new job and was asked to come in for an interview. She and I spent many sessions talking about going after career goals without the need for them to come to fruition in the way she expected, and this idea definitely began to take root in her heart and soul. Later that week, she called to tell me about the interview—what she'd done well and what she'd do differently the next time. She was excited about her possibilities, but not attached to getting the job. When she found out that she hadn't been offered the position, her mental preparation paid off in a big way. Instead of being devastated, she simply took it in stride and vowed to prepare more for future opportunities. She told me that this interview had been great practice for the right job that awaited her down the road.

It's clear that letting go of the end result doesn't mean that you can't still be motivated and excited when you pursue a goal. Personally, there's nothing I enjoy more than going after life with zest. Yet by letting go of the end result, you also let go of stress and disappointment. You change the way you see experiences so that "failure" becomes a lesson to help you grow, not something to devastate your desire and motivation.

Many incredible counselors with whom I've worked have encouraged me to keep focused on this important life philosophy, and by doing so I've reduced my stress levels and attained greater peace of mind. You can do the same in every area of your life, including the following:

Love

I once worked with a successful attorney named David who came to me with a relationship issue. He felt pressured to commit to a woman he'd been dating for a few years and needed help making the right decision. I sensed in his voice that he felt he had to make up his mind in a hurry— he was feeling that he might be keeping his girlfriend from her dream of having a family. I told David that I'd help him uncover the answers that he already had inside himself, but that he'd have to let go of the end result of our sessions— in other words, his need to find immediate answers to his questions.

Within minutes, something clicked inside David. He embraced the concept of letting go and released his need for fast answers, and I could see a physical and energetic change occur immediately. He relaxed and became completely comfortable in his own skin. He knew that whatever he decided, it would be the right path for him. The more he let go of having to know what the end result would be, the easier it was for him to know which direction he should go in. Life's answers came to him.

The concept of letting go of the end result could also benefit couples involved in divorce. I remember reading an article about a Florida politician and his spouse who, after five years in court fighting over the distribution of property, still hadn't come to a resolution. What a waste of energy, time, and money! While no divorce is easy, when you let go and trust life, you'll be more balanced and your healing can proceed at a record pace. Doubts about your ability to find new love in the future will diminish, and the bitterness and anger that you may feel can be released. Your desire to retaliate will fade away as you come to the understanding that your relationship wasn't meant to last. No matter what the outcome in court, with this mind-set, you win.

Work

Pamela came to me with a dilemma that was creating a lot of stress in her life. She wanted to leave her job, where she'd worked without fulfillment for 30 years, but she was afraid of what her father and friends would think, as she only had five more years to go before she'd qualify for a full retirement package. If she left now, she'd only get a percentage of those benefits, yet she desperately wanted to start a new career where she could help people heal in some way.

Pamela knew that to be happy, she had to make a move without attachment to a specific outcome. If she waited for everyone's approval and some kind of assurance that she wouldn't lose any income, she wouldn't make the change—regardless of how unhappy she was at her current job. She had to believe in herself and trust her instincts.

For many months, Pamela and I worked together, and she explored what was really important in her life. Her fears and worries diminished each month, and she knew deep down that her choice to make a career change was the right thing to do. Plus, looking at her situation objectively made her realize that with all her experience, she could always fall back on a job in her current field if she had to. So after taking an early retirement from her current employer, Pamela enrolled in school to become an acupuncturist.

When Pamela told her friends what she'd done, their responses were overwhelmingly positive. Her fear that people would tell her she was crazy to retire early never materialized. Instead, by letting go of the need for others to support her decision, she received their encouragement. Best of all, the person she was most concerned about disappointing—her father—was 100 percent behind her.

Yet the fact that everyone supported her was just icing on the cake. Pamela had slowed down, looked within, let go of the end result, and reaped a multitude of benefits for herself. Here's what Pamela had to say about her experience of letting go:

At first it was a struggle to leave the safety of the familiar, even though I knew it wasn't the right place for me. To walk away from the financial security of a well-paid position and jump into the unknown was scary, especially when I realized that the right path was not necessarily the easy path. Yet I've maintained faith that my needs will be taken care of, and the reaction I've gotten from friends and family has been a welcome surprise.

I don't know what the future holds, but the possibilities seem right. I feel that following the path to the healing arts and helping others is the reason I'm here on this physical plane of existence, and all my experiences help me heal others.

When we're strong enough to go after our goals and dreams and let go of our desire for approval, we prove our readiness to grow to the next level as human beings. We demonstrate that we're here to learn all life's lessons, which are often beautiful and unexpected.

Creativity

You may find that your creative abilities are enhanced when you aren't focused on how the results of your efforts will be rewarded. When I wrote my first two children's books, I had no attachment to how they might be accepted within the publishing community. I knew that these stories were given to me from a higher source, and I was happy to see my writing flow as it did. Of course I wanted the books to become huge bestsellers, but I didn't need that to happen to make me feel that they were a success.

, when I went to schools across the country to
ries, I hoped that kids would love the messages
m each one, yet I also knew that this didn't have
to happen for me to feel great about my work. The enthusiastic response I got from the kids was a beautiful blessing,
and the fact that Mark Victor Hanson (co-author of *Chicken
Soup for the Soul*), Jenna Elfman (star of TV's *Dharma &
Greg*), and Barbara Harris (editor-in-chief of *Shape* magazine)—as well as teachers and principals—all gave glowing
endorsements to these books was definitely an added bonus.
But I'd continue writing children's stories without such
recognition if I still had the desire to do so.

How about you? Are you holding back from pursuing
something very meaningful because you're afraid that the
end result may not be the one you envision? Know that your
creative skills will be enhanced if you release your need for
a specific outcome. Let go and pursue your dreams anyway.
It's the only way to live.

PUTTING THE "LETTING GO" THERAPY INTO PRACTICE

We never know how our experiences may alter our lives
for the better. But by letting go of what we feel we should
be getting from any experience, we open ourselves up for joy
and success in unexpected places. This philosophy has taught
me to look at my future—including intimate relationships
and career goals—in a new way, and now I'm always excited
about the endless possibilities. At the same time, I'm learning to let go of all the end results. In other words, while I
still want to find a fulfilling and deep connection with a
woman, I've released the need to have it happen with a
certain person, or type of person, by a particular date.

I have the same outlook with respect to my career—
it all, but I'm not attached to a specific outcome. As I m
into this mind-set, I release the stress that's so easy to create when things don't happen the way we think they should,
and I do my best to stay optimistic and unattached. Today
I dream big, work hard to achieve my goals, and then let go.

Now let's look at your life. Take some time to answer the
following questions:

- In the past, what goal have you wanted to go
  after, but hesitated pursuing because of your
  concern about what the end result would be?

  _____

  _____

  _____

  _____

- What end result for your actions and dreams do
  you need to let go of in the following areas?

  Love

  _____

  _____

  _____

  _____

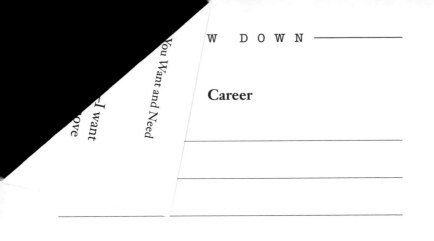

W   D O W N —————

Career

_____

_____

_____

_____

_____

Creativity

_____

_____

_____

_____

Other Areas

_____

_____

_____

_____

The less stressed we are, the easier it is to hear the wisdom within. The answers we seek come to us more readily when we're not asking them to jump up and reveal themselves. That's the power of releasing attachment to the outcome of the goals we set. Slow down, serve, and let go of your desired end result, and you'll find that freedom and success await you.

❋ ❋ ❋

Part VI Review

When you adopt a service-oriented mentality, set goals to assist others and yourself, and then go after all that you desire, you'll be sure to find the path that's right for you. When you combine that with a life philosophy that allows you to release your attachments, you open yourself up to accept the wonders of life in a way others only dream about.

Take a moment or two to slow down and review the information presented in Part VI. Remember that the writing exercises are truly the hidden gems of this work, and your written answers at the end of each part of this book will help you focus, create the intention to change, and then propel you forward as you set your action plan into motion.

The act of writing allows you to delve deeper into your mind to recall from the previous pages the information that was important to you and relevant to your life and desires. I believe that this is one of the many powerful steps that you can take in order to create the life you desire. So slow down, think, write, and then become who you truly want to be.

Please answer the following questions:

1. What was covered, in detail, in this section?

_____

_____

_____

_____

2. What was of most interest to you, and why?

_____

_____

_____

_____

3. What's the current plan of action you'll institute to help
you achieve your goal? (Specifically list the steps you'll
take to live the life you really want to.)

_____

_____

_____

_____

❋ ❋ ❋

Afterword

Now it's time for you to slow down and acknowledge who you are, what you want, and how you're going to achieve your most important dreams. Where do you need to be focusing your energies right now in order to be happier and more successful? In other words, where do you need to slow down? Do you need to show more gratitude for what you have? Do you want to expand your personal power, improve your physical health, or find ways to be of service to others? Perhaps you want to enhance your love life or spiritual side. Your answers lie within, and by now, I have a feeling that you know exactly where you're headed. Remember, *you* have the wisdom and power at this moment to transform your life and the lives of those around you. Never forget this truth.

There may be times when you slip back into your old ways of rush, rush, rush. When you notice this happening, simply repeat the mantra: "Slow down." You'll automatically be transported to a higher place—a place where faith, trust, and wisdom reside. It's all easily obtained, because you already have it.

I'm excited for your success, and I'm so happy that you're choosing to follow a new path, one that will surely bring to you all that you need and want. Slow down and cherish what you have in your life, and let go of what you don't have that you think you need. Now is the time to finally get all that you desire.

— With Love and Peace,
David

❋ ❋ ❋

Acknowledgments

As I slowed down to think of all the individuals I wanted to acknowledge, I was amazed by how much gratitude I have for so many people in my life. I'm a fortunate soul to be surrounded by people such as:

Ardith Bissinger, who dedicated herself to this project—and typed the complete manuscript over and over.

My brother, Terry; my sister, Marydianne; and her family, Bobby, Stacey, and Joshua—for their undying love.

Louise Hay, Reid Tracy, Danny Levin, Jill Kramer, Shannon Littrell, Katie Hammerling, Christy Salinas, Tricia Breidenthal, and everyone else at Hay House who knew that the message in this book would help the lives of millions.

My assistants Pat and Gary Nebel and Sheryl Duncan, who believe in me and this path.

All my lifestyle-coaching clients who have been so brave in their desire to grow personally through our work together, and my former national radio audience, who offered me so much with their love and support.

My friends, who have taught me much about love and life, including: Joe Cirulli, Armand and Frances Cirulli, Jeffery Meldon, Lee Witt, "Tall" Jim Schwartz, and counselors C J Moon and Merna Neims.

My cousins Gary and Louise Loughlin, and "Aunt" Mary and Uncle Louis for helping me in the loving way that they do.

Jean Westin, for her personal and professional guidance.

I'm so very appreciative for all the angels in my life and their continued guidance and support, which led to the writing of this book. If you don't see your name listed here, please understand that I do love you and your presence in my life.

❋ ❋ ❋

About the Author

David Essel is an author, lifestyle coach, speaker, and TV/radio host whose nationally syndicated motivational program was heard in more than 220 cities for nine years. An athlete, poet, and more, David has been labeled a "21st-century Renaissance man" for his ability to inspire millions through the combination of his creative, authentic, and philosophical energies and drive. His mission is to inspire others to reach their own personal potential, which now will be made easier through this book. David's professional presentations have drawn rave reviews from both Fortune 500 companies and school districts across the U.S.

❋ ❋ ❋

Hay House Titles of Related Interest

Books

An Attitude of Gratitude: *21 Life Lessons*, by Keith Harrell

BodyChange™: *A 21-Day Fitness Program for
Changing Your Body . . . and Changing Your Life!*
by Montel Williams and Wini Linguvic

Getting in the Gap: *Making Conscious Contact with God
Through Meditation (book-with-CD)*, by Dr. Wayne W. Dyer

Getting Unstuck: *8 Simple Strategies to Solving Any Problem*, by Dr. Joy Browne

Gratitude: *A Way of Life*, by Louise L. Hay and Friends

Inner Peace for Busy People: *52 Simple Strategies for Transforming Your Life*,
by Joan Z. Borysenko, Ph.D.

The Power of Intention: *Learning to Co-create Your World Your Way*,
by Dr. Wayne W. Dyer

A Relationship for a Lifetime: *Everything You Need to
Know to Create a Love That Lasts*, by Kelly E. Johnson, M.D.

Sacred Ceremony: *How to Create Ceremonies for
Healing, Transition, and Celebrations*, by Steven D. Farmer, Ph.D.

Shape Your Life: *4 Weeks to a Better Body—and a Better Life*,
by Barbara Harris, Editor-in-Chief, *Shape®* Magazine, with Angela Hynes

Card Decks

I Can Do It® Cards, by Louise L. Hay

Juicy Living Cards, by SARK

Manifesting Good Luck Cards: *Love and Relationships*,
by Deepak Chopra, M.D.

MarsVenus Cards, by John Gray

Tips for Daily Living, by Iyanla Vanzant

All of the above are available at your local
bookstore, or may be ordered by visiting:
Hay House USA: **www.hayhouse.com**
Hay House Australia: **www.hayhouse.com.au**
Hay House UK: **www.hayhouse.co.uk**
Hay House South Africa: **orders@psdprom.co.za**

We hope you enjoyed this Hay House book.
If you would like to receive a free catalog featuring
additional Hay House books and products,
or if you would like information about the
Hay Foundation, please contact:

Hay House, Inc.
P.O. Box 5100
Carlsbad, CA 92018-5100

(760) 431-7695 or (800) 654-5126
(760) 431-6948 (fax) or (800) 650-5115 (fax)
www.hayhouse.com

✳

Published and distributed in Australia by:
Hay House Australia Pty. Ltd. • 18/36 Ralph St.
Alexandria NSW 2015 • *Phone:* 612-9669-4299
Fax: 612-9669-4144 • www.hayhouse.com.au

Published and distributed in the United Kingdom by:
Hay House UK, Ltd. • Unit 62, Canalot Studios
222 Kensal Rd., London W10 5BN • *Phone:* 44-20-8962-1230
Fax: 44-020-8962-1239 • www.hayhouse.co.uk

Published and distributed in the Republic of South Africa by:
Hay House SA (Pty), Ltd., P.O. Box 990, Witkoppen 2068
Phone/Fax: 2711-7012233 • orders@psdprom.co.za

Distributed in Canada by: Raincoast
9050 Shaughnessy St., Vancouver, B.C. V6P 6E5
Phone: (604) 323-7100 • *Fax:* (604) 323-2600

✳

Sign up via the Hay House USA Website to receive the
Hay House online newsletter and stay informed about what's
going on with your favorite authors. You'll receive bimonthly
announcements about: Discounts and Offers, Special Events,
Product Highlights, Free Excerpts, Giveaways, and more!
www.hayhouse.com